Sutton Foster

From Broadway Sweetheart
to TV's Bunhead

A Children's Biography by
Christine Dzidrums

Sutton Foster

From Broadway Sweetheart
to TV's Bunhead

STAGE STARS

A Children's Biography by
Christine Dzidrums

CREATIVE MEDIA, INC.
PO Box 6270
Whittier, California 90609-6270
United States of America

www.creativemedia.net

Cover and Book design by Joseph Dzidrums
Front cover photo by Sylvain Gaboury / PR Photos
Back cover photo by ABC, Inc.

First Edition: Febuary 2013

Library of Congress Control Number: 2013933051

ISBN 978-1-938438-15-8   10 9 8 7 6 5 4 3 2 1

Thank you, Joseph,
for inspiring me to write this biography.

This book is dedicated to every young person who dreams of one day performing on Broadway.

TABLE OF CONTENTS

"My parents are very proud. All the money that they paid for all those lessons are going to good use."

THE UNIQUE SUTTON FOSTER
Chapter One

In 1974 a young married couple named Bob and Helen Foster lived in Georgia with their six-year-old son Hunter. Bob worked in sales for the American automotive corporation General Motors, while Helen, who once dreamed of being a model, became a full-time mother. The Fosters resided in Statesboro, a cozy college town. One day the tight-knit family discovered they were expecting another baby. Helen, who always disliked her generic name, vowed that the next Foster would bear a unique name.

On Tuesday, March 18, 1975, a joyous Bob and Helen welcomed a bouncing baby girl into their lives. They named their child Sutton Lenore Foster. A huge film buff, Helen heard the name in a movie once and always liked it.

At four years old, peppy Sutton often bustled about the family home seeking creative outlets for her limitless energy. The tiny dancer usually transformed the Foster's modest living room into a makeshift ballet studio while she practiced pirouettes, pliés and grand jetés. Eventually Helen enrolled her youngest child in a dance class at Augusta West Dance Studio. The baby ballerina loved the structured lessons, so jazz and tap dance classes also joined her blossoming schedule.

Flexibility plays a crucial role in attaining ideal dance positions. A naturally pliable child, Sutton already held a big advantage over her peers. However, the perfectionist constantly sought fresh ways to improve at her craft. Sometimes she would climb into bed at night and attempt to fall asleep while in the splits position!

A few months later, Sutton awoke early for her first ballet recital. She brushed her soft brown hair into a tight ponytail. Then the tiny dancer threw on white tights and a glittery blue leotard and laced up her favorite ballet shoes. She studied herself carefully in the mirror. Having lost her two front teeth recently, the conscientious youngster made a mental note to not smile. People might notice her toothless grin.

Sutton loved performing for the friendly audience, soaking up their applause during her bow. Her big eyes danced excitedly when she received beautiful flowers from her parents. It was official. The budding dancer adored show business.

When Sutton turned eight, the Fosters moved 80 miles to Augusta. Shortly afterward, the outgoing young lady appeared in her first play, *A Christmas Carol.* She played Ebenezer Scrooge's sister, Fan, in a community theater production.

A few years later, Sutton watched horrified as the United States space shuttle The Challenger exploded on live television 73 seconds after its takeoff. All seven crew members aboard died instantly, including teacher Christa McAuliffe, who dreamed of someday teaching students about her space travels. The tragedy prompted the small girl to change career plans.

"I really wanted to go to space camp," she recalled "After The Challenger exploded, I wanted to be an astronaut, because I thought people might be afraid, and I would be brave."

Sutton's plans eventually changed, though. One day she and a friend played in her upstairs bedroom. Suddenly her mother entered the play zone, clutching a community flyer.

"Do you want to try out for *Annie?*" Helen asked.

"No," Sutton answered. "I want to play with Bethany."

"She can come to the audition, too," Mom smiled.

Before the tiniest Foster realized it, she and her pal had piled into the family car and were headed to the town's local theater. When Sutton eventually walked onto the stage, the show's director asked her to sing something. The youngster shrugged nonchalantly then launched into an astonishing performance of "Tomorrow," the musical's signature song. Jaws dropped. The room fell silent in awe. Who was this dynamo? The small girl owned a remarkable voice.

Unaware of the impact she made, Sutton raced home from the audition to catch *Fraggle Rock* on television, hoping she might play the mean orphan Pepper in the musical. A few hours later, the unsuspecting girl received a shocking phone call. The director had cast her as Annie! She had never taken voice lessons, nor sung publically. Now she would play the lead role in a major production of a popular musical. The ten-year-old would sing the classics "Tomorrow," "Maybe" and "It's the Hard-Knock Life" every evening. Sadly, Bethany did not get cast in the show.

Sutton soon learned that huge responsibility accompanied a big role. Every day she arrived at the theater hosted in a barn and the director put her to work. There were lines, songs, choreography and stage directions to memorize. She even recorded a radio commercial advertising the show.

"I had the biggest Southern accent you'd ever heard," Sutton laughed when recalling the promotional spot.

UNIQUELY SUTTON
(Myra Wong)

Sutton also revealed herself to be a smart girl. Throughout the musical, Annie spends much time with her character's beloved dog, Sandy. On the rehearsal's first day, the wise youngster quickly befriended the animal actor. As a result, the dog never caused her any trouble throughout the show's run.

A very composed Sutton also ingratiated herself with *Annie*'s human cast members. Adults expressed awe and admiration for the little girl's professional demeanor. Many years later, actress Barbara Feldman raved to *The Associated Press* about the actress' remarkable composure at a young age.

"She walked in and she was perfect," she recalled. "She was so comfortable. She knew everybody's lines. And when the man playing Daddy Warbucks didn't stand where he should be, she had a way of nudging him into position."

On opening night, Sutton slipped on a red curly wig and examined her ratty costume. When the curtain rose, the natural performer captivated the audience as the tough but kind orphan who battles the evil orphanage owner Miss Hannigan. Later Sutton displayed her sensitive side when Annie learns her parents have died. By the show's end, though, a billionaire adopts the young girl, and she affectionately nicknames him Daddy Warbucks.

When the show's final joyful note played, the audience applauded heartily for the charming lead with the powerhouse voice. Sutton loved everything about musicals: the singing, dancing and acting. The new actress had only one question. Which show were they performing next?

"If you have the heart and the passion, just go for it."

"I CAN DO THAT!"
Chapter Two

Once Sutton discovered her strong voice, she flaunted it, singing for anyone and everyone. She also continued acting in local stage productions. Live performances thrilled her.

As fate would have it, the acting bug bit Hunter, too. Like Sutton, he owned a strong, steady voice and charisma to spare. The siblings often performed together and spent many afternoons discussing their Broadway dreams.

At age 12, Sutton auditioned for Augusta Community Theater's production of *Grease*, the comedy musical about angst-ridden high school kids in the 1950s. Hunter played Danny Zuko, Rydell High's cool greaser. His younger sister co-starred as overly-caffeinated cheerleader Patti Simcox.

Two years later, Sutton began classes at Troy High School. The school's reputable theater department produced quality shows and boasted a notable alumna, *A Chorus Line*'s Donna McKechnie. Meanwhile, the lanky 5'9" freshman strived to impress her drama teacher, Mr. Rick Bodick. All through high school, she grabbed every performance opportunity, appearing in dance competitions, music recitals and plays.

She usually aced auditions by singing *South Pacific*'s "Cockeyed Optimist" or "Oklahoma." Throughout the years, the plucky teen portrayed Frenchie in *Grease*, Guenevere in *Camelot* and Kristine, *A Chorus Line*'s scatterbrained dancer who can't sing. She even received her first kiss while playing

Ado Annie in *Oklahoma!* The versatile performer also appeared in the comedic play *You Can't Take It with You.*

Sutton loved musicals best, though. She spent every allowance buying Broadway cast albums, assembling an impressive collection. Her favorite recording? *Les Misérables,* a musical version of Victor Hugo's sprawling masterpiece chronicling Jean Valjean, an ex-convict seeking redemption in 18th-century France. The youngster played the CD endlessly, memorizing every song, each syllable, and every breath.

"Wouldn't it be cool to perform in the show someday?" she thought.

Sutton also considered herself a mini-couch potato. The Fosters watched wholesome situation comedies like *The Cosby Show, Growing Pains* and *Family Ties.* The teen also liked the cartoons *The Flintstones, The Smurfs* and *DuckTales.* She particularly loved singing the "Gummi Bears Theme!"

When Sutton turned fifteen, she made her television debut on the celebrated talent show *Star Search.* The outgoing youth competed in the junior vocalist category. Although she impressed viewers, future Broadway performer Richard Blake ultimately defeated her.

Sutton almost joined the *All-New Mickey Mouse Club* as well. After several lengthy auditions, she became a finalist for Disney's variety series revival but ultimately just missed making the cut. Meanwhile, the show produced several superstars: Britney Spears, Christina Aguilera, Justin Timberlake, Ryan Gosling and Keri Russell.

Despite pursuing major opportunities, Sutton lived an average teenage existence. During her junior year, she attended prom with her friend Jim Daley. She wore a red off-the-shoulder dress, white tights and a loose ponytail. She cherished her normal high school life and amazing friends.

That same year the Fosters vacationed in New York. The close family loved visiting the world's most famous city. Sutton even saw her first Broadway shows, *Miss Saigon* and *The Will Rogers Follies*. She dreamed of appearing on the Great White Way someday!

Once a year, Sutton reserved the television to catch The Tony Awards. She watched enthralled while the American Theatre Wing honored Broadway's best shows, actors and technical gurus. Three hours of musical numbers, glamorous stage stars and touching acceptance speeches mesmerized the budding actress.

The 1991 Tony Awards® especially wowed the sixteen-year-old. The memorable musical season featured a strong quartet. *Miss Saigon* followed a U.S. marine who falls for a bar girl during the Vietnam War. *Once on This Island* reimagined *The Little Mermaid* on a Caribbean island, and *The Secret Garden* musicalized the classic children's story about a spoiled girl coming of age. Finally, *The Will Rogers Follies* chronicled the comedian's life and career against the backdrop of the Ziegfeld Follies.

The four musical actor winners gave emotional, memorable speeches. *Miss Saigon*'s Jonathan Pryce and Hinton Battle took Best Actor and Best Featured Actor, respectively, while their co-star Lea Salonga won Best Actress. *The Secret Garden*'s Daisy Eagan won Best Featured Actress. Crying tears of joy, the pint-sized star became the award's youngest winner in history. As she struggled to regain her composure, organizers lowered an overhead microphone to accommodate her tiny height. The unforgettable moment would become Sutton's all-time favorite Tony memory.

During the Tony telecast, producers invited every Best Musical nominee to present a production number. *The Will Rogers Follies* cast, led by star Keith Carradine, performed the dance-heavy "Our Favorite Son," a tune chronicling the comedian's 1928 mock presidential campaign. Tommy Tune's grueling and intricate choreography would have challenged even the most seasoned dancer. However, when the routine ended, Sutton turned to her mother and confidently announced, "I could do that."

As fate would have it, the following summer *The Will Rogers Follies* held auditions for their national tour, and the driven seventeen-year-old attended the open call. The musical's co-choreographer Jeff Calhoun oversaw auditions. Because the show featured Ziegfeld showgirls, heavily made up women wearing revealing costumes dominated the holding room. Suddenly Jeff noticed one girl who looked different than the rest. Sutton wore a simple blouse, shorts, sandals and no make-up. The refreshingly natural look helped her stand out in the crowd.

Although Sutton lacked professional experience, her talent greatly impressed Jeff. She nailed the dance audition and sang like a dream. Floored by the teenager's raw talent, he offered her a coveted chorus role!

The enormous opportunity overwhelmed Sutton. The high school senior and her parents suddenly faced a huge decision. Should she leave school to tour with the show? After careful consideration, the determined teen accepted the gig. With only two credits remaining, she would finish high school via correspondence courses.

"I was reading *Teen Magazine* and *Sweet Valley High*!" Sutton later revealed to *BroadwayWorld.com*. "I didn't know how to be a showgirl - but I grew up very fast."

"I had a lot of tenacity. I just wanted it," she continued. "I thought I could do it and I did."

Sutton spent the next several months touring the United States. The youngest cast member, who could barely tolerate high heels, grew up quickly. Striving to make a positive impression with her first professional gig, she worked hard, kept her mouth shut and treated everyone respectfully.

YOUNG SUTTON
(Anthony G. Moore/PR Photos)

"It was pretty intense, traveling across the country by myself on my first time away from home and making the leap from local to professional theater," she later admitted to the *Chicago Sun-Times*. "But it prepared me for the rest of my career."

The Will Rogers Follies tour luckily hit Michigan during an ideal time for the high school senior. Although Sutton took correspondence classes, her bosses let her miss one performance to attend the senior prom. A few days later, organizers scheduled Troy High School's graduation ceremony in the afternoon, so she attended that event, too!

Shortly after graduating from University of Michigan, Hunter also won his first professional gig, joining the touring company of Andrew Lloyd Webber's epic musical *Cats*. As Rum Tum Tugger, the rebel feline loosely based on Mick Jagger, he sang several solos, including a frisky rock number. Hunter played the flirtatious role perfectly, catching the eye of fellow cast member Jennifer Cody, whom he began dating.

When her *Will Rogers Follies'* contract ended, Sutton returned home and enrolled as a theater major at Pittsburgh's Carnegie Mellon University. But although she liked the faculty and student body, she didn't learn anything particularly earth shattering. The professors taught stuff she'd already discerned while on tour. After completing two semesters, she left college and joined her parents who now resided in Memphis, Tennessee. Around the same time, Hunter moved to New York for more acting opportunities.

The restless teenager began working as a singing waitress at a Macaroni Grill. Although Sutton should have sung Italian arias, she sang show tunes instead. The rookie server wasn't great at her job, but she formed several lifelong friendships with her coworkers.

One day Sutton visited nearby Germantown, a historic railroad town east of the Mississippi River. On a leisurely stroll, she passed a children's community playhouse, Morgan Woods Theatre. Suddenly an overwhelming urge compelled her to knock on its front door.

"Do you need any help?" she asked a worker.

Understaffed theater volunteers eagerly accepted the generous offer. Once inside the building, Sutton surveyed the chaotic, creative and fun atmosphere. The playhouse was mounting a youth production of Cole Porter's classic musical *Anything Goes*. Before she realized it, the new volunteer scurried about the theater, building sets and sewing costumes. One afternoon the show's frazzled director approached her with an urgent question.

"Have you ever choreographed a show?" he asked.

A few hours later, Sutton, a novice at designing dance numbers, suddenly discovered nearly 40 eager children waiting for her guidance and direction. So the game artist simply did what she knew best. She threw herself passionately into the assignment, giving the kids 110% of her effort.

Several weeks felt like mere days. Sutton learned she could choreograph a dance-heavy show. The talented dancer also cherished working with youngsters, whose uninhibited enthusiasm warmed her heart. She loved the kids and they loved her.

On opening night, Sutton watched backstage beaming like a proud mom. Who cared that the children missed several cues or never mastered the dance steps? They had fun. That's all that mattered. The impromptu instructor adored her assignment. Was an educational career beckoning her? Should she return to college and earn a teaching degree?

Before she could further explore the idea, a phone call changed her life.

"Doing a show on Broadway is the dream I had when I was a little girl."

ANYTHING BUT MISERABLE
Chapter Three

Augusta Community Theater's former Danny Zuko played a supporting role in Broadway's *Grease* revival. Hunter missed his kid sister, though. Would she visit him?

While in Manhattan, Sutton stayed at her brother and sister in-law's apartment. Hunter had married Jennifer, also a *Grease* performer. Intrigued by her sibling's burgeoning career, the impressed sister grilled him about life as a Broadway performer. As he answered every question patiently and honestly, the actress realized she missed performing.

Replacement roles soon became available for *Grease*'s national tour. Equipped with her brother's priceless advice, Sutton attended an open call on a whim. Four days later, producers offered her a job. Before the performer realized it, she'd frantically packed her bags for rehearsals in San Francisco.

Grease follows two 1950s teenagers who find love one summer. Rydell High's slick greaser Danny likes goody-two-shoes Sandy Dumbrowski, but the lovers' different backgrounds provide complications. Can the young couple overcome their friends' disapproval and find true love? The musical's effervescent score featured many popular tunes.

Originally hired as an ensemble member, Sutton soon graduated to playing Sandy on the North American tour. Her co-stars included several celebrities. Television's Adrien Zmed headlined the show as Danny, 1980's singing sensation Debbie

Gibson played Rizzo, and Emmy winner Sally Struthers rounded out the cast as Miss Lynch. Despite the musical's famous résumés, critics routinely singled out the production's newcomer.

"Zuko fell hard for a girl over summer vacation, one Sandy Dumbrowski (played to saccharin-sweet perfection by Sutton Foster)." - *Chicago Sun-Times*

"Sutton Foster soars with her heart-wrenching rendition of 'Since I Don't Have You.'" - *Baltimore-Afro America*

"Sutton brings a welcome comic edge to the usually bland Sandy, as well as bouncy, blonde good looks that would fuel many a fevered teenage dream and a voice that would melt a 45-rpm down to a hunka hunka burnin' plastic."- *The Edmonton Sun*

A reinvigorated Sutton toured with *Grease* for 18 months. At one point, producers flew her to New York to play Sandy for a three-week engagement. The ingénue made her Broadway debut alongside Hunter. During the curtain call, she got goose bumps when taking her bows while holding her brother's hand!

A few months later, Sutton auditioned for a Broadway revival of *Annie*. When the determined actress walked onto the stage to sing "Oklahoma," she found herself looking directly into the eyes of the musical's director and lyricist, legendary Martin Charnin. Despite her nerves, she nailed the song and won a pivotal role.

When *Annie* opened on March 26, 1997, Sutton played the fittingly named A Star To Be. In a major production number "N.Y.C.," billionaire Oliver Warbucks and his assistant, Grace, take the orphan Annie out on the town. During their escapades, the threesome encounters a starry-eyed actress who arrives in Manhattan carrying enormous dreams. Every night the youngest Foster wowed audiences during her short but powerful moment.

Eight months later, Sutton joined the original Broadway production of Frank Wildhorn's *The Scarlet Pimpernel*. The action/adventure love story set during the French Revolution gained a small but loyal following during its New York stint. An ensemble member, Sutton played several roles in the show and felt thrilled to record the cast album.

On June 19, 1998, Sutton's childhood dream came true when she joined *Les Misérables'* Broadway cast. As she waited backstage for her first entrance as an ensemble member, the actress recalled playing the musical's recording over and over as a child. Was she really paid to perform in the show now? She played many parts, including a revolutionary student, whom she named Bob the Bullet Boy.

How Sutton wished she could play *Les Misérables'* major male roles! How about Inspector Javert, the strait-laced officer whose faith ultimately destroys him? After all, the character sang her favorite song, "Javert's Suicide." She would have also enjoyed playing Enjolras, the passionate student who inspires a revolt against the French government.

However, Sutton adored her assignment as the Eponine understudy. She'd long dreamed of playing the streetwise kid who worships the wealthy Marius, who loves another girl, Cosette. The spurned character sings "On My Own," a heart-breaking song that expresses the agony of unrequited love.

"I think that everyone knows how Eponine feels," she mused. "We have all loved someone who hasn't loved us back."

"Eponine has grown up on the streets and she sees what she doesn't have and she knows what she wants," the astute performer continued. "She always has hope. It's that hope that keeps her going. And she has incredible dignity for who she is. She won't let anyone tear her down."

Unlike most musicals, *Les Misérables'* script demands that its actors sing every line. Spoken dialogue does not exist. To ensure she kept her voice in tiptop shape, Sutton lived a quiet, low-key life. She also kept her mouth moist by drinking water and sucking sweet candies like Jolly Ranchers.

In early July, Sutton arrived at the Imperial Theatre for an evening performance. As usual, she began the process of slipping on her factory worker costume and applying her stage makeup. Suddenly the show's stage manager approached her.

"You're playing Eponine tonight," he announced.

Sutton felt overwhelmed, scared and excited. She would finally perform her dream role! With less than an hour to prepare, she raced to get her costume but discovered it had been sent out to be distressed (the costume crew always ensured the character's outfits looked properly worn and faded). The leggy actress frantically borrowed clothes from a more petite performer and attempted to make them fit. The mishap provided a good distraction. She had little time to think or get nervous before her character appeared on stage!

Casting agents initially considered the actress too tall for the role. However, Sutton's astonishing "On My Own" performance at her audition quickly changed their minds. The change of heart didn't stop the self-deprecating artist from joking about her height, though.

"I was the ginormous Eponine that terrorized the streets of Paris," she laughed.

At the beginning of 1999, Sutton became the primary Eponine in the Third National Tour of *Les Misérables*. Though the schedule was grueling, she enjoyed touring North America. In one month alone, she visited Mount Rushmore, the Grand Canyon and Niagara Falls. She particularly loved West Coast cities, like Portland, Seattle and San Diego.

"Playing Eponine is like some wild dream that came true," she remarked. "Every night I am still amazed that I am even doing it."

With such a demanding role coupled with constant travel, Sutton always headed back to her hotel room after a performance. She then changed into comfortable clothes and watched television. Her favorite shows included *Friends*, *Ally McBeal* and *Dawson's Creek*. And she preferred Joey with Dawson, not Pacey, thank you very much.

Sutton's *Les Misérables* gig offered some amazing perks. When the musical played an extended Washington D.C. engagement, then U.S. President Bill Clinton invited the cast to the White House's Independence Day party. The starstruck performer even shook the Commander in Chief's hand. Later she and her friends sat on the White House lawn, watching a brilliant fireworks show over the Washington Monument.

Although Sutton experienced much homesickness, the cast bonded like family. They always celebrated everyone's birthdays with a cake at intermission. The *Les Misérables* team even hosted their own Thanksgiving dinner. On one Halloween, they threw a big costume party, and Sutton dressed as a crocheting accident. For several hours, she walked around the gathering covered in fake blood with a crochet needle in her neck!

In December of 1999, the Les Misérables tour led Sutton to Los Angeles for a ten-week run. The actress loved the city, except its famous traffic jams! On Christmas Eve, the cast celebrated the holiday at Disneyland. Sleeping Beauty's castle adorned with Christmas lights made a majestic sight. The following morning, coworkers exchanged gifts through a Secret Santa program. Although the Michigan native embraced California's warm weather, it seemed strange wearing short sleeves on Christmas day.

While appearing in *Les Misérables*, Sutton cultivated a loyal fan base. Although many actresses had played the popular role, many felt she created a perfect blend of toughness and vulnerability that her predecessors had not achieved. Professional critics also admired her work.

"Eponine is played with heaping portions of youthful ferocity and anguish by Sutton Foster." - *The Washington Post*

"It was Ivan Rutherford (Jean Valjean), Todd Alan Johnson (Javert), and the lovely Sutton Foster (Eponine) who had everybody - including this columnist on Wednesday night - reaching for their hankies." – *The Washington Times*

"Both Stephen Bishop as Javert and Sutton Foster as Eponine were sharp in their roles and outstanding vocally, acting and singing with passion and exceptional skill." - *The Columbian*

Even wonderful things must end, though. On February 20, 2000, Sutton wore Eponine's trademark beret one final time. The performer loved playing the role, but after a thirteen-month run, she felt mentally and physically exhausted. So Bob and Helen's youngest child returned home and slept. A lot. She needed the rest. Her next role would lead her on a whirlwind journey that would make her one of Broadway's biggest stars.

COSETTE ILLUSTRATION
(Emile Bayard)

"I identify with (Millie's) tenacity to make a name for herself and create her own destiny."

THOROUGHLY MODERN MILLIE
Chapter Four

In early 2000, *Les Misérables'* producers offered Sutton the Eponine role in the New York production. The offer thrilled the young actress. She could secure a apartment and be a working Broadway performer. The job meant security, no travel and a steady income.

Except Sutton also eyed another role. For months she auditioned for the title role in the new 1920s musical *Thoroughly Modern Millie* and still awaited the producers' decision. San Diego's La Jolla Playhouse announced the show's pre-Broadway tryout, which would begin performances that fall. Finally her agent phoned with disappointing news. The talented ingénue Erin Dilly had won the role. Sutton knew the actress quite well, having worked with her as a child. She believed Erin would give a great performance.

Sutton also felt naturally disappointed, having desired the role greatly. She performed in the musical's early workshops and adored the show. Nevertheless, the young actress yearned to be part of the production in any capacity.

"I'd be willing to do ensemble," she told her agent. "Please call to see if they will let me in."

"I think you're making a mistake," her agent replied, nudging her to accept the *Les Misérables* offer.

"I don't know," she persisted, "I really believe in the show. There's something about it. I want to give it a shot."

Millie's producers reacted positively to Sutton's request. They offered her a small chorus role and Millie's understudy position, and she happily accepted both.

"I definitely wanted more, but I was always totally content with being in the ensemble," she later confided to the *Los Angeles Times*.

Thoroughly Modern Millie featured Jeanine Tesori's lively score and smart lyrics by Dick Scanlan, who also penned its hilarious script with Richard Henry Morris. Based on Universal Pictures' 1967 movie starring Julie Andrews, Mary Tyler Moore and Carol Channing, the upbeat musical follows a young Kansas girl named Millie Dillmount, who moves to New York, finds a secretarial job and pursues her rich boss. Along the way, while staying at an all-girls hotel, she dismantles an unscrupulous white slave operation and falls for her best friend, Jimmy.

One week before technical rehearsals, Erin became ill and Sutton temporarily replaced her. Despite learning the part in only three days, Sutton felt unusually relaxed and confident. In short, she finally nailed the role, impressing the show's commercial producers who caught a runthrough of the musical.

"When she stepped into rehearsal, something just clicked," director Michael Mayer told the *Los Angeles Times*. "She made sense of the role in ways that opened our eyes."

A few weeks later Sutton sat in her San Diego apartment thinking about the inevitable letdown. She cherished playing Millie but Erin would soon resume playing the title role. The actress felt understandably disappointed about returning to the chorus.

Then the phone rang.

Michael Mayer delivered major news. Erin was out. The creative team wanted Sutton to assume the title role. She could now portray Millie.

Sutton felt floored. She'd just been offered her dream role. First things first, she asked if Erin was all right. She admired the actress very much and hoped everything would be okay between them. As it turned out, her predecessor handled the crushing decision like a class act, never once blaming her understudy for the producers' decision.

"Erin and I have such a history together and there's no animosity between us," Sutton later told *Playbill*. "I think Erin is brilliant, one of the most talented actresses I know."

Once she realized the role was finally hers, Sutton wept - a lot. For four hours, the ingénue shed tears, unable to stop her uncontrollable reaction. She felt many conflicting emotions: joy, fear, and disbelief.

Some questioned the producers casting an unknown actress as the lead in a multi-million dollar show. However, the show's creators insisted it made perfect sense. Sutton's anonymity fit the role perfectly.

"The whole joy of Millie is that she's a girl from nowhere, out of place and determined to make her life in the city," Dick Scanlan told *The Record*. "Our concern is that if you cast a star, how could you have her say, 'I want to be somebody'? We felt that would undermine the whole premise."

Millie choreographer Rob Ashford felt ecstatic about his leading lady's dance skills. As a performer, he danced in Broadway productions like *Anything Goes*, *Crazy for You* and

Victor/Victoria. He held high standards for his dancers, and Sutton more than exceeded the show's demands.

"To have a leading lady who can dance your opening number down front, it's a dream," he raved to *Playbill*. "That doesn't happen very often. Sutton is that, with those long legs in the air, and she can do it. It's a treat."

Sutton also boasted steel lungs. A remarkable belter, her soaring vocals wowed the creative team. Except *Millie* didn't completely utilize their star's singing talents. The solution? A brand-new song. Jeanine Tesori and Dick Scanlan created "Gimme Gimme," a fiery declaration of love with a spine-tingling crescendo. Michael nestled the song near the show's climax when the title character must choose love or money. The rousing tune further strengthened the show's already strong score, and its leading lady knocked it out of the park every time she performed it.

Opening night felt like a wonderful dream. Sutton practically floated during the dance numbers, hit every song's notes and landed each joke. When the performance ended, the crowd rose enthusiastically, cheering musical theater's newest star.

"Opening night was one of the best nights of my life," she later recalled to *The New York Times*. "I was relieved and thrilled."

"Sutton Foster has certainly made the most of the opportunity with one of the most memorable characters I've yet seen," wrote *San Diego Playbill's* Rob Hopper. "Independent, intelligent, self-assured, and practical, but she's also hopelessly romantic, caring, and humorously awkward as a Kansan trying to look modern. Singing-wise, she especially shines in "Gimme Gimme," a song written specifically for her."

"As the titular heroine, young Foster tears into the part with earthy gusto," raved the _San Diego Union Tribune_. "She's got toughness and charm, and singing seven of the eight songs in the first act, she shows a rangy voice that won't quit. Add a perfect stage smile, a confident stride, and you've got a performer making the most of a big, brash role with Broadway potential."

The new Millie worked hard throughout the musical's California run, always giving audiences their money's worth. Sometimes, however, especially in live theater, mistakes happen. In Sutton's case, a certain flub became an embarrassing one that she would laugh about for years to come.

"I had to make a quick change during the opening number that took about 15 seconds or so," she recalled with a laugh. "I came back out, made the change, hit the final pose and my underwear fell down my ankles!"

Despite the minor gaffe, _Millie_'s San Diego run ended successfully. Months later, the cast began rehearsals for their Broadway opening. The musical's producers, the creative team and technical gurus worked daily implementing changes since the show's California debut. On a rare off day, Sutton attended the premiere of the ABBA jukebox musical _Mamma Mia!_, even walking the red carpet like a celebrity!

Remarkably, Hunter also conquered New York that season with _Urinetown: The Musical_. The satirical show chronicled a water-depleted city that bans private toilets. Hunter played Bobby Strong, a frustrated common man who leads a revolt challenging the city government's policy. Neither sibling took their Broadway careers for granted.

"It is hard to believe," Sutton remarked incredulously to *The Record*. "We just sort of look at each other."

Days before *Millie*'s Broadway opening, its leading lady strived to maintain focus on her show. Huge expectations rested on her tiny shoulders. She fought the impulse to drown in self-doubt.

"I have butterflies," she admitted. "I'm trying to keep my perspective, and focus on what I'm doing. I can't let myself think of other things, like the people I know from all over the country who are flying into New York to see the show. I'm trying to stay calm."

On the night of *Millie*'s last runthrough, Whoopi Goldberg sat in the theater studying the production carefully. One of the show's producers, the Oscar-winning actress worked tirelessly on the musical, citing a desire to mount an old-fashioned musical suitable for her grandchildren. Before the cast and crew left the theater that evening, the esteemed performer gave an impassioned motivational speech that left everyone in tears. A resurgence of confidence shot through Sutton. She suddenly felt eager to prove to the world that she could headline a Broadway show.

Finally opening night arrived, and ticket holders shuffled into the Marquis Theatre located in the heart of iconic Times Square. Cast members offered one another good luck hugs as they performed final vocal warm ups. The show's lineup featured many theater veterans, like Harriet Harris, Mark Kudisch and Sheryl Lee Ralph. Meanwhile leading man Gavin Creel headlined the newcomers making their Broadway debut.

Two and a half hours later, a deafening ovation greeted the show's final note. As each major player took their individual bow, the cheers grew louder and louder. When Sutton walked center stage, the applause rose to deafening decibels. Meanwhile, critics also loved the musical.

"Fun, funny and inventively staged. Sutton brings a mile-wide smile, nimble feet, and a belting voice to the starring role." - *Curtain Up*

"Foster is a fine singer and a bold comic presence." - *Variety*

"Bubbly as a glass of champagne _ domestic, not imported _ a bright, breezy American musical." - *The Associated Press*

"The biggest surprise of all is Sutton Foster who, in the lead role of Millie, had to contend with that bigger-than-life star Julie Andrews. But contend she did. Foster does much more than that. Her voice is vibrant, expressive and she exudes a charm and ease rarely seen in actors so young. She fits the role to the proverbial "T": she is the quintessential small-town girl who makes good in the Big Apple. In a few words, she is delicious." - *New York Beacon*

"(Sutton Foster's) got the full package: girlish gawkiness and Broadway brass, the legs and the lungs. Foster is a big reason the show is just about the cutest thing to hit Broadway since Annie's dimples, with perkily retro songs by Jeanine Tesori and clever staging by director Michael Mayer." - *Time Magazine*

Famous celebrities soon contacted Sutton. Television star Mary Tyler Moore wrote her a congratulatory letter, while Oscar winner Shirley MacLaine also wished her well. Meanwhile, Sutton's heroes, Julie Andrews and Carol Burnett, attended the show on separate occasions. Hollywood legend Warren Beatty also asked to meet the star after taking in a performance.

During her *Millie* run, Sutton lived a very reserved life. The physically taxing role demanded she exercise every ounce of her triple-threat talent. In response, she rested her body, voice and mind as much as possible and mostly stayed home during her days off.

Feeling she needed something more in her life, Sutton started searching for a hobby. On her birthday, she received a 25-gallon fish tank. She bought two goldfish, named them Sam and Henry and became quite the fish aficionado. The goofy actress even joined an online goldfish society and bragged shamelessly when her fish won pick of the week.

Sutton also watched her celebrity status skyrocket. It blew her mind that so many youngsters now idolized her. Every night when she left the theater's stage door, young girls waited for an autograph. Although the no-frills performer often visited with fans while wearing blue flannel pajamas and furry bunny slippers, the role model took her status very seriously. She happily gave advice to aspiring performers who asked for the key to her success.

"Take every opportunity you can," she told *BroadwayWorld.com*. "Try to learn as much as you can. Do shows, no matter what level it is. If you want to come to New York, don't limit yourself, meet as many people as you can. You

THOROUGHLY MODERN MILLIE
(Getty Images)

really have to believe in yourself and get yourself out there. Ask the world what you want. And tell the world what you want. I think a lot of people think they can't do this. You have to really believe that you can. People underestimate the power that they have."

When award season began, Sutton collected several neat souvenirs. For starters, she won The Astaire Awards' Best Female Dancer honors. Meanwhile, the Drama Desk and Outer Critics Circle named her Outstanding Lead Actress in a Musical.

The most prestigious award remained the Tony Awards, often called theater's Academy Awards®. On May 6th, the 56th annual Tony Awards® nominations would be announced live on television. Because Sutton didn't expect a nod, she never set her alarm.

But she couldn't sleep. She spent the night tossing and turning. Finally, at 8:20 a.m. she clicked on the television. Actors Jennifer Jason Leigh and Steven Weber stood in famed Sardi's restaurant ready to read the nominees.

Best Performance By A Leading Actress In A Musical

Sutton Foster
Thoroughly Modern Millie

Nancy Opel
Urinetown

Louise Pitre
Mamma Mia!

Jennifer Laura Thompson
Urinetown

Vanessa Williams
Into the Woods

Best Musical

Mamma Mia!
Sweet Smell of Success
Thoroughly Modern Millie
Urinetown

All in all, *Millie* led the pack with 11 Tony nominations, while *Urinetown* and Stephen Sondheim's *Into the Woods* revival took 10 notices each. Sutton's cast members, Gavin Creel, Mark Kudisch and Harriet Harris, received recognition, too. Voters also acknowledged the show's score, book, direction, costumes, choreography and orchestrations.

Sutton's nomination thrilled her. More importantly, she loved seeing so many of *Millie*'s artists also recognized. The first-time Tony nominee celebrated by riding Toys r Us' iconic 60-foot indoor Ferris wheel.

"The coolest thing about the day was all the phone calls I got," she told *The New York Times*. "People from all over the country. Emails galore, my cell phone, my home phone, just tons."

"I got emails from old friends and high school friends' parents emailing me," she continued. "Parents of college friends sending me email. I got more phone calls the day the Tony nominations came out than I did opening night."

A few days later, Sutton visited *The Today Show* and performed *Millie*'s title song. Afterward then host Katie Couric interviewed Sutton. The pair discussed her ascent to the role, the *Thoroughly Modern Millie* movie and the upcoming awards. Throughout the interview, Sutton kept calling Katie "ma'am."

"You don't have to call me ma'am," the anchor laughed. "I'm not that old."

"My mother will kill me if I don't call you ma'am," the well-mannered artist giggled shyly.

When Katie mentioned Sutton's actor brother, his younger sister smiled proudly. She stressed that the two didn't have any sibling rivalry. They always wished each other well and would be happy if either of their shows won the Best Musical Tony.

"As far as I'm concerned, it's a win-win situation," Sutton smiled. "I'm so proud of him and everything that he's accomplished."

Even *People Magazine* interviewed the Foster children. The weekly publication featured the dynamic duo in an article entitled, "Sis, Bro and Broadway." The siblings showed their support and admiration for one another throughout the feature.

"I'm rooting for my sister and for *Urinetown*," Hunter declared diplomatically.

Broadway legends Bernadette Peters and Gregory Hines hosted the 56th Tony Awards®. A dazed Sutton waved at adoring fans cheering from the street before she headed into Radio City Music Hall. The leggy entertainer once dreamed of being a member of the Rockettes, a world-famous precision dance team who perform at the legendary venue. It seemed her dream had nearly come full circle.

Sutton later achieved her fantasy of dancing on the famed stage when she and *Millie* cast members performed a medley from their show. They thrilled the audience with the rousing tap routine "Forget About the Boy" and the title song. When the number ended, the audience applauded loudly while television cameras caught Michael Mayer beaming and cheering.

Meanwhile, *Urinetown* enjoyed a great evening when the musical took best book, score and directing honors. Hunter also led the show's ensemble in a terrific performance to "Run Freedom Run." After the number finished, cameras showed his sister sitting in the audience smiling and applauding proudly.

Finally Sutton's category arrived. Jerry Orbach and Doris Roberts walked onto the stage and announced the nominees for Best Actress in a Musical. The Tony newbie sat calmly waiting to hear *Mamma Mia!*'s Louise Pitre's name called as the winner.

"And the Tony Award goes to Sutton Foster!"

Wearing a black, lacy Badgely Mischka dress, a stunned Sutton waited a few seconds to let the shock wear off. Then she stood and headed toward the stage. On the biggest night of her life, five words kept running through her mind.

"Don't trip on your dress!"

Although the victory surprised Sutton, she delivered an eloquent speech.

"To say that this is a dream come true is an understatement. I could not be more honored to be a part of this show. It is truly a thrill to work with this incredible company every night. I want to personally thank the entire creative staff and the producers for trusting their work, to take a risk on hiring me. I want to thank my parents for all of their support and encouragement to follow my dreams. My incredible brother, Hunter Foster, for his unbelievable friendship. All of my teachers, Joan Leder, Joan Rosenfeld, my high school drama teacher, Mr. Bodick, who is here tonight! Thank you! My dresser, Julien Havard, my agent Steven Unger, oh my gosh, my beautiful boyfriend Christian, our incredible stage manager Bonnie. Thank you so much! Thank you."

After Mary Tyler Moore presented Best Musical to *Thoroughly Modern Millie*, Sutton spent the night and early morning celebrating with her colleagues and friends. When she finally arrived home at 4 a.m., a sign decorated her apartment building's front door.

"Congratulations to our new tenant, Sutton Foster, on winning a Tony Award."

Once inside her apartment, Sutton smiled while listening to nearly 40 congratulatory voice messages. Before she went to sleep that night, the self-professed nerd looked around her apartment scrupulously. Her Tony award needed a good home. She finally placed the trophy on her computer desk next to her Darth Vader and Darth Maul action figures.

MEGAWATT SMILE
(Anthony G. Moore/PR Photos)

"(Jo's) a huge dreamer and she never takes no for an answer. She defies all the odds and breaks all the rules."

LITTLE WOMEN
Chapter Five

One evening Sutton sat in her *Thoroughly Modern Millie* dressing room absorbed in a script. Songs from the Broadway-hopeful *Little Women – The Musical* played softly in the background. Tears crept down the actress' face while the show's breathtaking songs and timeless story overwhelmed her. In that moment, Sutton yearned to play literary heroine Jo March.

Composer Jason Howland and lyricist Mindi Dickstein musicalized the beloved children's classic *Little Women*. Louisa May Alcott's semi-autobiographical Civil War-era novel chronicled the trials and tribulations of the young March sisters: aspiring writer Jo, sensible Meg, shy Beth and spoiled Amy. Sutton eagerly agreed to a read-through for director Susan H. Schulman and the show's producers. Within minutes of the informal reading, the actress immediately clicked with the character.

"I sat down at the table and started reading, and I didn't have to 'work,' or 'try,' I just was her," she recalled. "I thought, 'If I turn this down I'll regret it for the rest of my life.'"

Several months later, *Little Women*'s creators were ready to debut their show but faced one problem. Sutton still had contractual ties to *Thoroughly Modern Millie*. Rather than cast a different actress, they waited for their first choice to fulfill her prior commitment.

When Sutton's *Millie* run eventually ended, she focused on *Little Women* by reading the novel several times. Then she watched all three film versions: George Cukor's 1933 Katharine Hepburn version, Winona Ryder's 1994 Oscar-nominated turn and June Allyson's spunky 1949 portrayal. Singing Jo liked the latter adaptation best.

"I liked that version because I could see a musical in it," she told *Broadway.com*. "It was very theatrical, and I could see where musical numbers could be inserted in the story."

A few weeks later, Sutton traveled to Concord, Massachusetts. When she arrived in the historic town, she headed straight to Orchard House, the Alcott family home where Louisa May wrote her famous novel. The actress also visited the author's grave at Sleepy Hollow Cemetery, vowing to honor her story.

Sutton felt honored and excited to play Jo, the driven tomboy. Like she did in *Millie*, the actress headlined the show as a plucky heroine. She also expected that audiences would draw comparisons between the feisty characters.

"Though they have different landscapes, they're both these headstrong young women trying to break out of the chains of tradition," Sutton told *Playbill*. "That's still true for so many women today. I mean, to live in a world where there hasn't been a female President of the United States? Even in the 21st century, *Little Women* speaks to me. Even though it was written in 1868, it was so before its time."

A formidable cast joined Sutton in the show. International recording star Maureen McGovern portrayed beloved mother Marmee. Meanwhile, Jenny Powers depicted

Meg, Megan McGinnis breathed life into Beth and Amy McAlexander played Amy.

Sutton's reunion with Megan thrilled her. They'd become best friends when sharing the stage in *Thoroughly Modern Millie*. For Sutton, it seemed natural to portray Jo's protective attitude toward her buddy's sickly character.

"She's my best friend," Megan gushed to *Broadway.com*. "But who doesn't love Sutton?"

Songs form a musical's emotional foundation. Fortunately for *Little Women*, Howland and Dickstein penned a lovely, diverse score. Sutton would sing several group numbers, the buoyant "Five Forever" and two show-within-a-show pieces that told stories sprung from Jo's creative pen. A heartbreaking duet, "Some Things Are Meant to Be," showed the writer reluctantly accepting her sister's imminent death. Meanwhile, her two solos included "Astonishing," a soaring anthem chronicling Jo's longing to break free from traditional gender roles and the tender "The Fire Within Me" when the sister in mourning rediscovers her writing passion.

On a brisk September afternoon, Sutton stood nervously on stage at Broadway on Broadway, Times Square's free outdoor concert. *Little Women's* producers took advantage of the event to debut their first act finale, "Astonishing." Nerves ran through the singer's body. Her heart pounded in her throat. Ultimately, though, she nailed the song, while the dazzled crowd offered a huge ovation.

"She's always terrified," Hunter smiled. "And then she's always amazing."

Before *Little Women*'s Broadway run, producers scheduled an out-of-town tryout at the Reynolds Theater on the Duke University campus. In fall of 2004, Sutton wowed the opening night audience. The musical's director expressed wonderment at her leading lady's dynamo performance.

"I knew how talented Sutton was, but I wasn't expecting to be amazed," Susan raved to *Playbill*. "She's fearless!"

"Foster is a gem," declared *The News & Observer*. "It takes mere moments to fall in love with her Jo, a delightful blend of gawkiness, candor and charisma. Her voice is pure and strong. Her acting feels genuine and focused. And her physicality is brilliant in comedic and sober moments alike."

Following *Little Women*'s successful preview period, the company returned to New York and began preparations for its Broadway run. Sutton celebrated the holidays heartily and even made a few resolutions.

"I want to take better care of myself," she told *Broadway. com*. "Eat better, see friends more and maybe buy a new goldfish!"

Unfortunately Sutton developed bronchitis after the new year and missed a week of performances. She utilized the down time by learning the show's most recent creative alterations. The actress also reflected on her new project.

"I'm really proud of the show," she told *Broadway.com*. "Ultimately, whether the reviews are glowing or critical, I still have to perform the next day. I just want to hold on to my own feelings of pride. My responsibility is to do a good show. I feel very strongly about that."

Little Women officially opened at the Virginia Theatre, now the August Wilson Theatre, on Sunday, January 23, 2005. As fate would have it, the same building previously housed Hunter's Tony-nominated turn in the classic musical *Little Shop of Horrors*. Rosie O'Donnell, Matthew Morrison, and The Monkees helped celebrate the premiere. Following the opening night performance, wearing a glorious red halter gown, Sutton partied with cast and crew at the Central Park restaurant Tavern on the Green.

"The present production, skillfully staged by Susan H. Schulman, is full of delightfully calculated performances, including an entrancing turn by its giddily attractive star, Sutton Foster as Alcott's deliciously hoydenish, proto-feminist heroine, Jo." - *New York Post*'s Clive Barnes.

"You couldn't wish for a more ideal choice than Foster to play the gangly Jo March. She's got the acting, singing and dancing chops to nail the physical and emotional demands of the character and the music." - *Curtain Up*

"Sutton Foster has found an ideal follow-up vehicle for her Tony-winning triumph in *Thoroughly Modern Millie*. (Foster is) a stronger performer than ever, supremely confident and always in charge. The role fits her like a glove." - *Broadway. com*

Ghostlight Records preserved *Little Women* via a cast album. On the momentous recording day, Sutton entered the studio wearing a green t-shirt, brown jacket and blue jeans. A simple ponytail held back her soft brown hair. She battled anxiety and nerves.

"I was really nervous when we first started," she admitted to *Broadway.com*. "Now I'm having more fun!"

"You always are nervous because you're thinking, 'oh this is forever,'" she added. "I don't have the chance to do this again so you hope that you're at your best."

Despite some positive notices, *Little Women*'s box office numbers ultimately struggled. Several months after its premiere, producers announced that the musical would end its run. Although the closing notice prompted a ticket sales surge, as theatergoers rushed to catch the production before it turned off its lights, the show closed on May 22, 2005, after playing 137 performances.

Little Women's early closing didn't hurt Sutton's award recognition. She received Drama Desk, Drama League and Outer Critics Circle nominations. The popular star also won *Broadway.com*'s Audience Choice Award for Favorite Leading Actress in a Broadway Musical and Favorite Diva Performance.

On the morning of the Tony Award nominations, Sutton crawled out of bed at 8:27 a.m. She clicked on the television for the live announcements. Finally, the main acting categories arrived.

Best Performance by a Leading Actress in a Musical

Christina Applegate
Sweet Charity

Victoria Clark
The Light in the Piazza

Erin Dilly
Chitty Chitty Bang Bang

Sutton Foster
Little Women

Sherie Rene Scott
Dirty Rotten Scoundrels

LITTLE WOMEN
(Getty Images)

Sutton smiled excitedly at her second Tony nomination. It always felt wonderful when voters acknowledged her work. However, she was also sad that her performance represented *Little Women*'s lone nomination.

"I'm disappointed that the show and its creators didn't get recognized in the way that I think they should, but it's an unbelievable season and it's a thrill to be part of such an exciting time on Broadway," she told *Broadway.com*. "I love *Little Women* so much. I'm excited to wear something pretty on Tony night."

On June 5, 2005, Sutton arrived at Radio City Music Hall for the 59th Tony Awards®. She wore a stunning Michael Kors' yellow-and-white floral gown and borrowed Harry Winston jewelry. Her chic outfit made several best-dressed lists.

As expected, Victoria Clark took home Best Leading Actress in a Musical for her touching performance in *The Light in the Piazza*. Meanwhile, Sutton just felt happy to be at the Tony Awards. She told reporters earlier that her presence at the awards proudly represented *Little Women*'s entire team.

When presenters announced the final Tony Award recipient, Broadway's 2005-06 season officially ended. And so did Sutton's *Little Women* journey. She would remember the experience with great fondness and always carry a bit of her character with her.

"I think more than any other character I feel closest to Jo March," Sutton said simply.

ANIMAL LOVER
(Jon Gilbert Leavitt)

"Millie was gawky, a colt. Janet is a show horse who knows her dressage."

THE DROWSY CHAPERONE
Chapter Six

One day while taking a walk, Sutton encountered former *Thoroughly Modern Millie* cast member Casey Nicholaw and they became absorbed in a conversation. Her friend now enjoyed a successful second career and would soon direct *The Drowsy Chaperone*, an original comedy musical set to premiere at Los Angeles' Ahmanson Theatre. Suddenly Casey stopped speaking, looked thoughtfully at Sutton and uttered seven words she would never forget:

"There's a part for you in it," he proclaimed.

When Sutton eventually read *The Drowsy Chaperone* script, she loved the hilarious tale with a big heart. Featuring Bob Martin and Don McKellar's witty book, music by Greg Morrison and Lisa Lambert's lyrics, the show billed itself as a love letter to 1920s musicals. Within the show's first few minutes, the audience meets a lonely man obsessed with vinyl records, especially a musical called *The Drowsy Chaperone*. Man in Chair, as he's called, describes the show to the audience, and its characters come to life in his living room.

Sutton agreed to play Janet Van De Graaf. In the show within the show, her character, a Broadway star, abandons her successful career to marry her dream man. The cast also included Georgia Engel, Bob Martin, Edward Hibbert, Eddie Korbich and Beth Leavel.

"The show is really special," Sutton gushed to *Broadway. com*. "Being part of an original production that celebrates musical theater is exciting. It's funny, sweet, smart, touching and completely different for me. I'm excited for audiences to see it."

But Sutton nearly missed the Los Angeles engagement. Less than two weeks before the show's first performance, she took a spill during rehearsals and broke her wrist. Fittingly enough, the injury happened during the runthrough of a production number called "Accident Waiting to Happen." Insisting the show must go on, Sutton and Casey restaged certain details to accommodate her temporary handicap.

Sutton's especially loved one thing about *The Drowsy Chaperone*. Unlike her previous two musicals, she was not the star of the show belonging to a very talented ensemble instead. The prospect of not being the sole person under a bright spotlight appealed to the performer.

"I love it," she confessed to *Playbill*. "I wanted less to do. *Millie* was very demanding, and I thought that *Little Women* was going to be less, and it ended up being the same amount of workload, and I was burned out. I was very close to taking a long time off, and then this came along."

"I feel completely satisfied without being completely depleted," she added.

On opening night Sutton and her co-stars stood in the dark backstage listening to Bob Martin begin the first scene. The audience roared at the musical's first line, "I hate theater." Immediately, the ensemble relaxed, sensing people would embrace the show's quirky humor.

That theatergoers cheered *The Drowsy Chaperone* shouldn't have surprised anyone. In a jukebox musical era, audiences simply adored an original story that featured loveable characters, big laughs and hummable tunes.

Critics also liked *The Drowsy Chaperone. Variety* praised the score, singling out Sutton's big song, "Show Off." *TheaterMania.com* gushed about the musical's script, acting, direction and production values. *Los Angeles Times* called it, "an unabashed love letter not just to musical comedy but to those romantic souls for whom show tunes are a daily form of worship."

Once news of the show's raves reached New York, a Broadway transfer seemed inevitable. The musical even won five L.A. Ovation Awards including Best Musical in a Large Theater and acting trophies for Sutton and Bob Martin.

A rousing success, *The Drowsy Chaperone* ended its Los Angeles run on December 21st and promptly booked Broadway's Marquis Theater for an open run. Sutton then spent the holidays with her family and boyfriend Christian Borle, a Broadway actor appearing in Monty Python's *Spamalot.*

A strong musical boasts one showstopping song that leaves the audience humming as they exit the theater, and *The Drowsy Chaperone*'s big number, "Show Off," belonged to Sutton. In the cheeky tune, Janet expresses disinterest and disdain for the spotlight. Yet throughout the hilarious song, she performs various stunts that clearly draw attention to herself. She juggles, performs an impressive quick change, pulls a Houdini, dive rolls through a hoop and executes cartwheels into the splits.

"Casey was asking me what tricks I could do," Sutton explained to *Playbill*. "I said I could do cartwheels and splits and kicks. I could do stuff when I was a kid, [and he said], "Do you think you could go back and take lessons?" I was petrified. I thought, 'Well, I'm not in dancer shape,' so I got a trainer, went to Chelsea Piers and took lessons."

Sutton began a one-on-one class with a private gymnastics coach. Some days she blushed when finding herself surrounded by ten-year-olds performing fancy tricks, like back handsprings. Despite her embarrassment, she worked diligently and had a blast.

"It was a really fun thing to do," she continued. "I had never done anything like that, and for some reason I was deter-

SHOWING OFF
(Getty Images)

mined to try to achieve something. It's so exciting to be doing all these things I did when I was a teenager."

The Drowsy Chaperone opened in New York on May 1, 2006. Audiences flipped for the high-spirited show, and critics loved it, too. Everyone also gave high marks to the entire cast, including the musical's leading lady.

The New York Times' Ben Brantley enthused that Bob Martin and Sutton gave "entrancing performances." Howard Kissel of *The New York Daily News* declared, "(The show is) full of wit and high spirits." *Variety's* David Rooney called it "a witty valentine from musical theater lovers to the frothy tuners of the 1920s." Finally, Michael Kuchwara of *The Associated Press* urged, "If you want to get some idea of what it means to be over the moon for musical comedy, pay a visit to Broadway's Marquis Theatre, where a disarming, delightful soufflé called *The Drowsy Chaperone*, is making a strong case for song-and-dance obsession."

Fifteen days after *The Drowsy Chaperone's* opening, Sutton awoke at 8:30 a.m. Bleary eyed, she crawled out of bed, snuggled on her living room sofa and turned on the television. Tony winners Phylicia Rashad, Natasha Richardson and Liev Schreiber gathered at Lincoln Center's New York Public Library for the Performing Arts to read the 2006 Tony Award nominations.

Sutton's heart beat quickly. She didn't anticipate an acting nomination for herself but longed for *The Drowsy Chaperone* to receive due recognition. She cherished the show and hoped others would also embrace it.

Best Performance by a Leading Actress in a Musical
Sutton Foster
The Drowsy Chaperone
LaChanze
The Color Purple
Patti LuPone
Sweeney Todd
Kelli O'Hara
The Pajama Game
Chita Rivera
Chita Rivera: The Dancer's Life

Sutton couldn't believe her ears. They nominated her? As a member of the ensemble, she didn't expect anyone to single her out. Regardless, the humble actress felt honored to be acknowledged in a category packed with so many legends. Before she could celebrate, though, another category caught her attention.

Best Musical
The Color Purple
The Drowsy Chaperone
Jersey Boys
The Wedding Singer

The Drowsy Chaperone garnered 13 total nominations, the most for any show that season. Her co-stars Bob Martin, Beth Leavel and Danny Burstein also received nods. Before she could fully absorb the good news, her phone began ringing with calls from friends, industry professionals and various media outlets. Her email box also overflowed with well wishes, and she received several floral deliveries.

"I never thought that I would be a Tony contender. I was flabbergasted, thrilled and really excited for our show," Sutton told *Playbill*. "They kept saying *Drowsy Chaperone, Drowsy Chaperone*, and by the end I was up on the couch wide awake. I tried to go back to sleep, but I couldn't - I was so excited."

The craziest thing about Sutton's nomination? Her long-time idol, Patti LuPone, Tony winner for *Evita*, also earned a Best Leading Actress in a Musical nomination. The stunned nominee expressed disbelief at sharing the same category with her childhood hero.

"When you're a kid growing up, you don't ever think that you would ever even be listed in the same sentence as her, so that's really surreal," Sutton told *Playbill*. "I admire her so much, and she's so brilliant in *Sweeney Todd*."

"It's a fantastic cast, and it's a real joy to come to work," Sutton continued. "It's a great place to work. I feel like the nominations honored every aspect of the show. It's not just one person. A whole slew of people have poured their heart and soul into it."

As the theater season continued, *The Drowsy Chaperone* accumulated several more victories. The Drama Desk and the New York Drama Critics Circle awarded it Best Musical honors with Sutton also scoring nominations. In addition, "Show Off" won *Broadway.com*'s Favorite New Broadway Song category.

On June 11, 2006, Sutton walked the red carpet for the 60th Tony Awards®. She wore a gorgeous spaghetti-strapped halter gown by American fashion designer Randi Rahm. Later that evening, Sutton led *The Drowsy Chaperone* team in a much-heralded performance to "Show Off." Although Sutton did not take home a trophy, the production claimed five honors, including Best Book of a Musical and Best Score.

The Drowsy Chaperone's ticket sales soared following the Tony broadcast. Producers then announced a national tour.

Professional productions popped up all over the world including Japan, Australia and London. Talks of a film starring Oscar winner Geoffrey Rush as Man in Chair ran rampant. The show's success didn't surprise Sutton, who believed the show's universal themes touched many people.

"Everybody has something that takes them away or makes them happier," Sutton mused to *Playbill.* "To some people it's baseball or sports or knitting or the movies. Everybody has something that when they're feeling blue, they can pull out their favorite comic or film. Man in Chair says — all he wants is to be entertained and to be taken away for a couple of hours, and this musical does it for him. I feel like this show validates everyone's passions, whatever that passion is."

Sutton also filmed three episodes of *HBO's* acclaimed comedy series *Flight of the Conchords.* The cult hit followed New Zealand musicians, Bret and Jermaine, who move to New York to pursue stardom. *The Drowsy Chaperone* star played Coco, a professional sign holder who catches Bret's eye. Before long, television's new star found that people recognized her just as much from *Conchords* as her stage career!

While Sutton's professional career flourished, her personal life blossomed, too. On September 18, 2006, Sutton married longtime boyfriend Christian Borle. Fittingly, the ceremony took place on a Monday, a day when most Broadway shows turn off their lights. The clever scheduling allowed the couple's many acting friends the opportunity to attend the wedding without requesting vacation days. Sutton's parents, now Cape Canaveral residents, flew to New York for the wedding, and their daughter cherished their presence.

SUTTON AND BOB MARTIN
(Janet Mayer/PR Photos)

"They don't get a chance to come up to New York a lot," she told *Playbill*. "They support from afar and are avid readers of all the things on the Internet, and they really keep up with everything. I wished that they lived closer. They live so far away."

Following a two-week honeymoon, the newlyweds purchased a two-bedroom apartment in mid-town Manhattan. Feeling somewhat domesticated, Sutton yearned for her own pet. Although she loved cats, her allergic reactions to them prevented her from adopting one. The actress instead became a first-time dog owner, adopting a black and white Shih Tzu. She named him Linus, after the blanket-toting Peanuts character.

Sutton worshipped her family addition, taking him to the theater every day, where he stayed in her dressing room. Linus even accompanied his mom on vacations and business trips. She taught him to sit, stay, shake and high five. Like his owner, the much-loved dog possessed endless energy.

The creative artist also explored the visual arts, completing several paintings for her personal collection. She even donated four holiday cards to Broadway Cares' charity organization. Her popular artwork depicted various snowmen acting in the smash hit musicals *The Phantom of the Opera, Les Misérables, Wicked* and *The Drowsy Chaperone*.

"I love to experiment with all sorts of things, collage, pen/ink and acrylics," the talented artist told *EdgeBoston.com*. "I just love to create, and I love to create art."

Sutton also began a book club. As the president, the loyal Kindle owner invited only her closest female friends, and the group met every six weeks to discuss a chosen book. They sipped wine and ate delicious food until the wee hours. The women studied many notable works, including Gilda Radner's autobiography *It's Always Something*. A proud bookworm, the avid reader considered John Irving's *A Prayer for Owen Meany* as her favorite book.

It came as no surprise then when Sutton lent her vocal talents to a special literary project, narrating the audio version of the classic children's book *Betsy-Tacy*. In Maud Hart Lovelace's 1940 semi-autobiographical work, little Betsy Ray befriends her new neighbor, Tacy Kelly. The title character

spends many afternoons telling amazing stories to an enchant-
ed Tacy.

As Sutton narrated the famous work, she had no idea that
a fresh stage opportunity lay around the corner. Nearly 2,500
miles away, an Oscar-winning comedian worked diligently on
his eagerly awaited Broadway musical. He would soon offer the
young actress one of its leading roles.

"I found my way in with Inga by thinking of her as a simple farm girl. We both come from simple backgrounds. She's from Transylvania and I'm from a small town in Georgia."

YOUNG FRANKENSTEIN
Chapter Seven

Several years earlier, Sutton and her friends celebrated Halloween during *Little Women*'s North Carolina tryout. Suddenly someone suggested the group watch Mel Brooks and Gene Wilder's film comedy classic *Young Frankenstein*. The room responded with giddiness and anticipation.

"I've never seen it," Sutton confessed.

"What?" her friends exclaimed. "Are you kidding us?"

Sutton nodded in mock shame. She had watched Brooks' *Space Balls*, a *Star Wars* parody a lot. However, she had never seen his popular film about a neurosurgeon who inherits his grandfather's monster creation.

Her friends excitedly popped the DVD into a player. No sooner had the first dialogue begun than the group started reciting the movie's well-known lines alongside the actors. Sutton laughed heartily throughout the film. By the time The Creature performed a song and dance routine to "Puttin' on the Ritz" while donning a top hat and tails, she declared it one of the funniest movies she'd ever seen.

A few years later during *The Drowsy Chaperone*'s run, Sutton sat eating dinner with her dresser Julien when her phone rang. The caller ID listed her agent's name. She answered her cell immediately.

"Hello?" she asked.

MEL BROOKS, SUSAN STROMAN AND ROGER BART
(Janet Mayer/PR Photos)

"Mel Brooks is doing a workshop of his next musical, *Young Frankenstein*," her agent stated. "They want you to play Inga."

"What?" she exclaimed. "Are you serious?"

Sutton stared at her phone for a second after the conversation with her agent ended. Then she shrieked happily, jumping up and down with glee. Julien looked quizzically at his best friend.

"What?" he asked. "What? What?"

"I just got asked to be a part of *Young Frankenstein*!" she announced triumphantly.

Sutton felt floored that they considered her for the blonde bombshell lab assistant. Immortalized on screen by Teri Garr, the memorable character delivered some hilarious lines. The wacky part would make a terrific stage role.

Susan Stroman, who served as director and choreographer for Mel Brooks' previous musical *The Producers*, would provide double duty on *Young Frankenstein*, too. Meanwhile Mel wrote the show's music and lyrics, and he shared the book credit with Thomas Meehan.

The workshop's first day appropriately fell on Halloween. Cursed with a nervous stomach, Sutton battled anxiety when she entered the room. The apprehensive actress smiled after being greeted by a pumpkin sporting a Frankenstein face. When Mel Brooks spotted his leading lady, he introduced himself and kissed her cheek. His kind nature relaxed the actress, and the musical's test run went swimmingly.

A few years later, after Sutton appeared in several of the show's workshops, Mel finally announced the musical's Broadway run. *Young Frankenstein* would play Seattle first. Then it would hit New York several weeks later. They offered Sutton the Inga role for the full-blown production, and she happily accepted.

Young Frankenstein's cast boasted impressive résumés, including Tony winners Sutton, Roger Bart (Dr. Frederick Frankenstein), Shuler Hensley (The Monster) and Andrea Martin (Frau Blücher). Rounding out the all-star squad, Emmy winner Megan Mullally played Elizabeth, Fred Applegate portrayed Kemp and Christopher Fitzgerald provided laughs as Igor, the hunchback assistant

Expectations ran high for the forthcoming musical. Coming on the heels of Mel's previous smash *The Producers*, theatergoers expected another high-quality production. Sutton believed the creative team would meet the challenge.

"This movie is so iconic, well known and beloved," she admitted. "We've all spent time studying the original and then bringing as much of ourselves to it as possible. The show does a really good job of toeing that fine line of paying respect and keeping all those classic moments but then surprising the audience by bringing brand new elements. I think we're doing a really good job."

Throughout the musical's preparations, Sutton constantly shook her head in amazement. Despite starring in several major Broadway productions, she'd never taken part in a grand spectacle. The show's 16-million-dollar budget allowed for impressive lighting and sound effects rarely used in live theater. Such enhancements helped the show create an appropriately creepy mood. During one rehearsal, a burst of thunder startled the actress so much that she screamed out loud!

Young Frankenstein held its first Seattle preview on a warm August day. The musical played the cavernous 2700+ seat Paramount Theater, a landmark building on the National Register of Historic Places. A delighted audience attended the show's debut, ecstatic to catch a Broadway-bound show.

"It was amazing," Sutton recalled to *Playbill*. "I've never been in a show that had so much anticipation. We stood at the end of the show, and the response was so extreme that it just negated itself. I have nothing to compare it to, so it flipped back to zero, and I stood there drooling with my mouth open. I didn't know how to take it all in."

After the show's official opening, the artists celebrated at the Space Needle, the city's landmark 605-foot observation tower. *The Seattle Times* posted a mostly favorable review proclaiming, "Staged by Stroman with impressive fluidity, given its heft, *Young Frankenstein* has a cast of expert merrymakers; shtick galore; winning dance numbers; elaborate sets by Robin Wagner that are marvels of seamless stage technology; and all the explosions, fog and wowie lighting effects (by Peter Kaczorowski)."

Sutton soon discovered that her popularity extended outside New York's borders. When she exited the stage door nightly, fans waited for an autograph, a photo opportunity or a few minutes with their idol. The flattered actress cheerfully obliged each request.

In her spare time, Sutton explored historic Seattle. The Emerald City offered several legendary attractions, such as Puget Sound, Pike's Market, the original Starbucks and Mount Rainier. The Pacific Northwest's jewel claimed a spot in Sutton's heart as one on her favorite cities.

Meanwhile back in New York, Hunter prepared for his own Frankenstein experience. He would soon star as mad scientist Victor Frankenstein in the off-Broadway musical *Frankenstein*, a serious take on Mary Shelley's classic novel. As a child, he adored the monster series.

"This role excites me," Hunter told *Broadway.com*. "It's like nothing I have done and I am thrilled for the challenge."

"I think that it is a crazy awesome coincidence that we are both going to be in two different Frankenstein shows at the same time," Sutton added. "I'm so happy for him and can't wait to see it!"

As bombshell Inga, Sutton sported a different look than her usual wholesome self. The self-confessed tomboy appeared nearly unrecognizable on stage. She wore sultry dresses, dangerously high heels and a blonde wig with luxurious locks.

"I've never felt more beautiful," she confessed.

While working on *Young Frankenstein*, Sutton cherished collaborating with her idols. A strong presence throughout the show's progress, Mel attended every rehearsal and preview performance. At first, the smitten actress kept her distance from the comedic genius, not wanting to bother him. However, she quickly learned that he possessed a sweetheart nature and became fast friends with him. On one occasion, it blew her mind when she realized she was having dinner with the legendary Mel Brooks!

BROADWAY SWEETHEART
(Sylvain Gaboury/PR Photos)

"It's great to work with Mel Brooks," the performer told *Dance Magazine*. "He's iconic and a legend and yet he knows my name and says hi!"

Sutton also delighted in working with Susan Stroman, Broadway's acclaimed director and choreographer. The esteemed artist captured Tony Awards for *The Producers, Crazy for You* and *Contact*, all shows that Sutton loved. Sometimes she felt like a fan girl, often arriving early for rehearsals merely to watch Susan choreograph musical numbers that didn't even involve her character.

"She uses everyone's strengths," Sutton gushed to *Playbill*. "She wants to make you feel amazing. She's so supportive. I love her, and I admire her so much, but I also think she's unparalleled with what she can do with a musical number and what she brings out of people. I'd work with her again and again and again. I hope I get to."

A brilliant song and dance girl, Sutton found herself front and center during the show's most thrilling group numbers, like "Transylvania Mania" and "Puttin' on the Ritz." However, she also sang two memorable solos.

For her introductory number, Sutton performed "Roll in the Hay," which introduces Inga in a ridiculously fun way. As Frederick gets driven to his late grandfather's house, his new assistant surprises him with an impromptu hayride. Throughout the number, the carefree spirit dances and yodels for him all while navigating the moving vehicle.

"I'm underneath some hay in the wagon for about a minute and a half before I pop up," Sutton told the *New York Daily*

News. "And then every night I get to perform this fantastic number. You rarely get to yodel these days on Broadway."

In the second act, the manic action slows as Inga expresses feelings for her boss in "Listen to Your Heart." Mel actually wrote the number after he realized his leading lady needed more stage time in act two. The tune became the composer's favorite song in the show.

A few months later, *Young Frankenstein* celebrated its Broadway opening on November 8, 2007. The musical's first performance attracted many notable names: Walter Cronkite, Mike Nichols, Billy Crystal, Goldie Hawn, Martin Short, Rosie O'Donnell, Regis Philbin, Natalie Portman, Mike Wallace and Gene Wilder. Despite a malfunctioning staircase, the show's debut went exceedingly well, and its audience responded with hearty cheers and applause.

After the premiere performance, cast, crew and select invitees partied at the Empire State Building. Guests discussed the show as they sipped wine, ate fine food and enjoyed private access to the 86th floor observation deck. By late evening, critics weighed in with their thoughts, and Sutton's performance received rave reviews.

"Sutton Foster is delicious as Dr. Frankenstein's voluptuous young assistant. The deadpan friskiness of her "Roll in the Hay" is a high point." - *The New York Times*

"Sutton Foster is the best she's ever been as Frederick's bombshell assistant Inga." – *TalkinBroadway.com*

"(Sutton) has a daffy sexiness that's nicely understated, and her hilariously staged "Roll in the Hay" number with yodeling chorus is a high point among Brooks and Thomas Meehan's often interchangeable songs." - *Variety*

"The show gets captivating work from Sutton Foster (the yodel-happy Inga) and rising star Christopher Fitzgerald (a relentlessly goofball Igor)—to say nothing of TV's Megan Mullally, who sings the daylights out of the Madeline Kahn role." - *New York Magazine*

AS INGA IN YOUNG FRANKENSTEIN
(John Sibley)

"Sutton Foster yodels spectacularly as Inga, the shapely lab assistant." - *Entertainment Weekly*

Sutton's performance brought her much attention. She sang "Roll in the Hay" with Roger and Christopher on *Late Show With David Letterman* to great acclaim and participated in a photo shoot for *Vanity Fair* magazine. Sutton even amassed award recognition for her performance. She received a Drama League Distinguished Performance Award nomination, and she and Roger won *Broadway.com*'s Audience Award for Favorite Onstage Pair.

Still an enthusiastic theatergoer herself, Sutton attended several different shows that season. A variety of musicals like *The Little Mermaid*, *Passing Strange* and *Xanadu* highlighted a bustling theater year. However, she particularly admired the work of Lin Manuel Miranda, *In the Heights'* lead actor, composer and lyricist.

"I think he's a genius," Sutton remarked. "He is so wonderfully engaging in that show. He's so inspired. It was such an incredible performance. I think he's wonderful."

All in all, *Young Frankenstein* provided Sutton with many terrific experiences. She'd met heroes, created friendships and proved she could play against type as a fetching blonde with superior yodeling skills! As she strolled down the streets of New York contemplating taking a well-deserved vacation, she bumped into Jason Moore, former resident director on the *Les Misérables* tour. He was preparing to direct a brand new musical by *Thoroughly Modern Millie* composer Jeanine Tesori.

"Have you ever played a princess?" he asked.

"Playing Princess Fiona has been such a joy. The whole experience has been fantastic. We're reaching audiences of all ages. I feel so lucky to be part of it."

SHREK THE MUSICAL
Chapter Eight

Based on the 2001 animated movie, *Shrek the Musical* follows a green ogre who rescues Princess Fiona just in time for her wedding to the deplorable Lord Farquaad. On his life-changing journey, Shrek finds love, befriends a wisecracking donkey and encounters several other beloved fairy tale characters. The musical features David Lindsay-Abaire's clever book and lyrics, and Jeanine Tesori's irrepressible score.

For the original Broadway company, Brian d'Arcy James assumed the title role made famous on film by Mike Meyers, while Sutton played Fiona, a part created by Cameron Diaz. Christopher Sieber sunk his teeth into the villainess Lord Farquaad and John Tartaglia portrayed Pinocchio. The very talented ensemble included Hunter's wife, Jennifer Cody, whose perky presence energized the Broadway shows *Cats*, *Beauty and the Beast* and *The Pajama Game*.

Like she did with *Young Frankenstein*, Sutton flew to Seattle for *Shrek*'s tryout. The New York-bound musical booked the 5th Avenue Theater for a nearly month-long run. The historic theater hosted past pre-Broadway tryouts *Jekyll & Hyde*, *Hairspray*, and *The Wedding Singer*. The actress loved the venue, having previously performed there while touring with *Les Misérables* and *Grease*.

"(It's) possibly the most beautiful theatre I have ever played," she once gushed.

Shrek played its world premiere performance on August 14, 2008. Theatergoers turned out in large numbers to see the Broadway hopeful. When asked by *Playbill* to describe Seattle audiences, the actress gave them high praise.

"(They were) amazing," she remarked. "Really receptive, very encouraging, very supportive, and also very discerning."

Critics gave thumbs up to *Shrek*, citing its strong book, music and lyrics. They also extolled the show's top-notch production values like its scenic design, lighting and costumes. The stellar cast, including its lead actress, gathered many accolades. All in all, the show was off to a great start.

The Seattle Times wrote, "It's a treat to have inimitable Sutton Foster as Fiona, the princess Shrek rescues, then falls for. Underutilized in the 2007 Seattle debut of Broadway's *Young Frankenstein*, here Foster has a better vehicle for her comic verve and sparkling singing — starting with "I Know It's Today," a fetching song about getting impatient for that promised knight in shining armor to arrive."

Variety gushed, "Foster is beautiful and plucky — at times bordering on the berserk, giving you the sense that anything could happen at any moment."

Shrek's creative team skillfully used the preview period to make changes that would strengthen the show. They even listened attentively to audience feedback by deleting one of Sutton's solos and penning an alternate finale. For the record, the amenable star embraced both decisions, expressing a desire to produce the strongest show possible.

Believe it or not, *Shrek* provided a first for Sutton. Her past roles included a flapper, a writer, an actress and a pauper. For the first time, though, she played royalty.

"She's not your typical princess," Sutton laughed while talking to *Playbill*. "She's a little bipolar, but rightfully so. She's been locked in a tower for 20 years. She's grown up, like we all have, with ideas of how the world works. She's surrounding herself with fairytales, and that's what she's trying to emulate. She's trying to be this perfect princess, but ultimately she is struggling with her inner ogre. She really finds herself when she meets Shrek."

Sutton thrust herself into the part by role-playing with cast members. She also watched Disney films like *Sleeping Beauty*, *Cinderella* and *Beauty and the Beast*. Although the actress enjoyed playing a beautiful princess, she stressed that the role ran deeper than esteemed lineage and good looks.

"Looking out in the audience and seeing little girls dressed up with crowns on their heads," she continued. "I love what they've done with the musical in that they've deglamorized that a bit. We show Princess Fiona literally trapped in a tower. It's like, 'This isn't actually as romanticized as I imagined.' She's trapped in there for 20 years going crazy!"

Shrek demanded only one thing that Sutton didn't enjoy. In the popular story, Fiona transforms from a bewitching princess into a green ogre. Every night, when makeup artists approached the actress with green sponges to apply her new coloring, she jokingly recoiled in horror.

On December 14, 2008, *Shrek* opened at the Broadway Theatre, where Sutton had seen her first New York show, *Miss*

Saigon. Stars who attended the big performance included Cameron Diaz, who later congratulated Sutton, Joan Rivers and *Ugly Betty's* America Ferrera.

The old-fashioned musical charmed critics. "*Shrek the Musical* is sweet, big and extremely lovable," raved *Newsday's* Linda Winer, while *The Associated Press* declared, "the folks at DreamWorks have done their darndest to make sure we are entertained at *Shrek the Musical,* the company's lavish stage adaptation of its hit animated movie."

As it had on the West Coast, Shrek opened to kudos from several critics. Sutton especially garnered strong notices with many naming Fiona's "Morning Person" as the showstopping song. They also praised her witty performance and robust comedic timing.

"(Sutton) has emerged as an inspired, take-charge musical comedian in the tradition of Danny Kaye and Carol Burnett." - *The New York Times*

"Foster (gives) a hilarious performance that gets better and better as the show goes on." – *Variety*

"Princess Fiona (is played by) the perfectly cast, perfectly perky Sutton Foster." - *Entertainment Weekly*

A few weeks later, *Shrek* recorded its original Broadway recording. Although the morning and afternoon session ate into the cast members' day off, they felt delighted to immortalize the show. All their performances would live forever through CDs and digital forms.

"I think the score is so fantastic," Sutton raved. "I can't wait to record it."

Meanwhile, Sardi's honored *Shrek*'s leading lady on March 3, 2009. Known for its Broadway caricatures lining their walls, the famed eatery unveiled a Sutton Foster work. Past legends honored with the tradition included Yul Brynner, Robert DeNiro, Douglas Fairbanks, Katharine Hepburn and Liza Minnelli.

Sutton arrived at the busy restaurant looking gorgeous, wearing a breezy blouse in her favorite color - yellow, a dark skirt and stunning black boots. She cheered exuberantly upon seeing her drawing. Then she autographed the piece and posed for media photos while cradling the work.

"It sort of feels like I've made a name for myself in my chosen field," she remarked modestly.

"I thought the teeth would be bigger," she laughed. "It's awesome. It looks just like me. It's an honor. That people took time out of their day to come and support me takes my breath away."

"I don't know where (the caricature is) going to live," she continued cheerfully. "I'll have to come check out where it's

FIONA, DONKEY AND SHREK
(Getty Images

WITH BRIAN D'ARCY JAMES
(Sylvain Gaboury/PR Photos)

hanging. I'd love to come and ask for the Sutton Foster table and have some steak and potatoes."

Meanwhile back at the theater, *Shrek*'s ensemble rehearsed a late addition to the score. The musical's creative team inserted The Monkees' classic song "I'm a Believer," heard prominently during the film, in the show's curtain call. Sutton loved singing the popular tune, often mentioning the four-member group as a major musical influence.

While performing in *Shrek*, Sutton spent hours crocheting in her downtime. She always gifted finished works to friends. Whenever the Broadway star created a new piece, she often lounged in her apartment wearing comfy clothes while watching television's *Grey's Anatomy*, *America's Next Top Model* and *Project Runway*. For a while she became absorbed in the ABC drama *Lost*. Whenever the show got especially juicy, the excited fan ran to her refrigerator for a bowl of ice cream, preferably Breyers' Vanilla Bean Hershey chocolate syrup or Ben and Jerry's Oatmeal Cookie Crunch.

Sometimes Sutton caught a matinee at a local movie theater. One afternoon she watched the Julia Child biopic *Julie and Julia* and resolved to cook more often. A film buff, she enjoyed escaping into engrossing movies. Her favorite movie was *Sense and Sensibility* starring Emma Thompson, Kate Winslet and Alan Rickman. She also loved *Dead Poets Society*, *Forrest Gump* and *Almost Famous*.

Despite telling a fairy tale nightly, Sutton's personal life suffered when she and Christian ended their marriage. Nevertheless the couple handled the split with class and dignity. Years later, when asked to name his favorite Broadway performance, her ex-husband didn't hesitate to answer.

"Sutton Foster in *Thoroughly Modern Millie*," he replied quickly. "It was one of the most amazing things I've ever seen on stage. To be with her while all that great stuff was happening was my great honor."

Upon the start of award season, *Shrek* and Sutton received repeated recognition. The show won twelve Drama Desk Award nominations including a nod for its leading lady and a victory for Brian. Sutton also received a Drama League nomination and shared the Outer Critics Circle's Best Actress in a Musical with *West Side Story*'s Josefina Scaglione. She even took *Broadway.com*'s Audience Award for Favorite Diva.

"I don't think I'm a diva," she deadpanned. "I need to work on it. I demand chocolate."

Unlike previous years, Sutton skipped watching that year's Tony nominations' broadcast. Instead she took Linus for a walk and then grabbed some coffee. As she headed back to her apartment, a friend sent her a congratulatory text. A minute later her agent called.

"Did the show get nominated?" she asked anxiously.

"Yes," he replied.

Best Musical

Billy Elliot the Musical
Next to Normal
Rock of Ages
Shrek the Musical

Sutton sighed, relieved. She loved the musical and felt grateful to see it recognized with theater's highest honor. The show received eight total nominations, including acting nods

MEETING CAMERON DIAZ
(Janet Mayer/PR Photos)

for Brian and Christopher. To her surprise only, the respected actress also picked up the fourth nomination of her career.

Best Actress in a Musical

Stockard Channing
Pal Joey
Sutton Foster
Shrek the Musical
Allison Janney
9 to 5
Alice Ripley
Next to Normal
Josefina Scaglione
West Side Story

"I desperately wanted the show to be nominated," she reacted tearfully. "I believe in it. I care about all the people that created it, and I wanted it to be recognized. I think it deserves to be. I felt relief. I could not care less if I was nominated. I just wanted the show to be."

Although *Next to Normal's* Alice Ripley took home Best Leading Actress in a Musical, Sutton made a big splash at the 63rd Tony Awards®. Accompanied by Hunter, she wore a stunning orange gown while walking the pre-show red carpet. She and *Shrek's* cast then kicked off the telecast with a buoyant performance to "Freak Flag," a tune celebrating uniqueness.

When her *Shrek* experience ended months later, Sutton expressed gratitude for supportive coworkers and a diligent creative team. She felt honored to have played the fiery Princess Fiona who proves that beauty is only skin deep. The down-to-earth actress adored the show's positive message.

"I think it's a great role model to young girls to embrace your inner ogre and [know] that beauty really is within and not necessarily what you look like," she told *Playbill*. "I think that's a really important message."

WITH BROTHER HUNTER
(Sylvain Gaboury/PR Photos)

"(Wish) is a very personal expression of me."

WISH
Chapter Nine

Sutton might have mastered show tunes but she loved many musical genres. The singer's iPod featured an eclectic range. Bon Iver, Peter Gabriel, Ingrid Michaelson and Patty Griffin were just some artists who dominated her playlist.

After years of anticipation, Sutton released her debut solo CD *Wish* in 2009. Presented by Ghostlight Records, the work showcased a jazz-infused mix of Broadway, cabaret and pop songs. The album even included Jeff Blumenkrantz's original tune "My Heart Was Set on You."

Sutton embraced every aspect of the CD's production. She chose each song, created the cover's artwork and requested that *Thoroughly Modern Millie* lyricist Dick Scanlan pen the CD's liner notes. His beautiful ode began with the fitting sentence, "If the song list is eclectic, so is the singer."

"(The songs) had to speak to me lyrically," she told *TheaterMania.com*. "We wanted to introduce songs people didn't know and to unearth hidden gems. I didn't want it to be predictable or just a CD of Broadway tunes -- like Sutton belts all the classics. I wanted it to be a window on who I am as a person and as an artist. I know you can't please everyone, so I tried to please myself."

Sutton and Megan McGinnis also recorded a song together. The best friends reimagined Craig Carnelia's "Flight" as a duet, showcasing beautiful harmony on the aching tune about life's longings. When asked if she had any future dream collaborations, Sutton supplied a quick answer.

"I'd love to do a duet with my brother, Hunter," she smiled.

Sutton even recorded a song by country singer-songwriter Patty Griffin. Although she adored her idol's entire song catalogue, she chose the haunting "Nobody's Crying" about a woman who has recently lost a loved one. The tune marked her biggest challenge because she admired Patty so much and hoped to do her song justice.

Wish thrilled music lovers, especially Sutton's fans, many who purchased the CD on its release date. Critics also praised the strong work. *Playbill* raved, "Foster invests whatever she's singing with a lyrical intelligence and a sunny alto that can caress notes or belt them to the rafters with equal ease."

"I was actually nervous about putting the CD out," she told St. Louis' *Riverfront Times*, "I worried that people might expect me to only sing brassy Broadway songs. But ultimately this material and these lyrics are the truest representation of what I wanted to say at the time. Now the CD is out, and people have received it very well. So that's a lesson: You can't lose if you listen to the truth in yourself."

Sutton also launched her first national tour, *An Evening with Sutton Foster*. The show, which premiered on February 4th in St. Louis, featured Broadway tunes and songs from her debut CD. Before the beloved actress sang a single note, she received a spontaneous standing ovation from her audience.

"Ms. Foster is more than just a pretty face and spectacular voice," wrote *Cabaret Scenes Magazine*. "On stage she radiates a self-effacing cheerfulness that's instantly charming and demonstrates the solid acting skills you'd expect from someone with her résumé." *Chicago Tribune* praised her "remarkable mix of steely determination, pitch-perfect sound and girl-next-door vulnerability." Meanwhile, *Backstage.com* declared, "Beat the drums for the thoroughly irresistible Foster. A new cabaret star is born."

The show's big highlight occurred when Sutton held a red binder labeled *The Big Book of Reeeeeally High Belt Songs* and asked a random audience member to select her next tune. Among the classic song choices? "Defying Gravity" from *Wicked, Dreamgirls'* "And I Am Telling You" and "Meadowlark" from *The Baker's Wife*. Each unique crowd seemed delighted with the opportunity to select the stage star's next song.

When Sutton arrived in Los Angeles for a gig, she received the full celebrity treatment. For starters theatergoers helped make her show at the Kirk Douglas Theater a sell out. *Los Angeles Times* then wrote a hefty article profiling Broadway's bright talent. When describing her concert, the goofy actress quipped, "It's definitely quirky and weird -- and very much me."

In one self-effacing moment in the show, Sutton addressed a major celebrity moment for her. Months earlier her name appeared as a question on a popular game show. As usual, she elicited laughs at her expense.

"Guess what?" she asked the audience. "I was a question on *Jeopardy!* I didn't see it but a friend of mine saw it. He's like, 'Sutton you really made it when you're a question on *Jeopardy!*' But then he told me that none of the contestants knew the answer."

The acclaimed act drew raves and packed concert halls. Nevertheless Sutton always felt nervous before taking the stage. Performing her cabaret show exposed a newfound vulnerability.

"You're not hiding behind any character," she explained to the *Los Angeles Times*. "Sometimes you want to ask, 'Where's my wig?' You're literally being yourself. And that's the hardest part."

Her cabaret concert proved so popular that Ghostlight Records released a CD preserving the show, *An Evening With Sutton Foster – Live at the Café Carlyle*. Recorded at New York City's legendary hotel, the album's song list included Broadway standards and several obscure, inspired selections.

During this time, Sutton also became a New York University professor. While teaching four classes, she especially enjoyed running a 15-week course entitled "Song Performance Workshop: From Rodgers to Heart." During the class, the Broadway star taught her students the art of selecting the right song and connecting with an audience. At the workshop's conclusion, students performed their pieces at the historic Joe's Pub.

"(Teaching has) been life changing," she marveled. "I absolutely love it so when my schedule allows it, I hope to be able to continue and teach there."

Sutton performed for an ultimate audience herself when she sang in consecutive years at the Kennedy Center Honors. Hosted by former First Daughter Caroline Kennedy, the performing arts lifetime achievement award honors inductees annually before a star-studded crowd that includes the U.S.

President and First Lady. Sutton felt honored to sing in the 2010 Jerry Herman tribute and 2011's Barbara Cook induction.

That's right. Award organizers now flew the Michigan native to D.C. to perform for the President of the United States. It wouldn't be long, though, before a former American president would travel to Sutton himself. After all, like so many others, he clamored to witness Broadway's biggest star give the most acclaimed performance of her career.

Sutton Foster Wish

DEBUT CD

"I'm excited to be in a big Broadway musical again, with tap dancing and all those old fashioned songs. It's the role of a lifetime, and I'm excited to put a new spin on this musical that so many people love."

ANYTHING GOES
Chapter Ten

In early 2011 musical theater fans rejoiced when Roundabout Theatre Company announced a mounting of Cole Porter's *Anything Goes* starring Sutton Foster. The beloved musical originally debuted on Broadway in 1934 starring Ethel Merman. Fifty-three years later Patti LuPone headlined Lincoln Center's acclaimed revival.

Anything Goes tells the timeless story of Reno Sweeney, an evangelist-turned-nightclub singer, who finds love during a trans-Atlantic cruise. The memorable score features such classics as the title tune, "You're The Top," "It's De-Lovely," "Blow, Gabriel, Blow" and "I Get a Kick Out of You."

"Reno is a character who seemingly has everything," Sutton told *Playbill*. "She's a star, and she has her own club, and she has men all over her, but she doesn't have love, and the guy that thrills her loves someone else."

When producers first approached Sutton about playing the role, she jumped at the chance. Seconds later, though, she changed her mind. The conscientious performer suddenly wondered if she could achieve the high standards set by the show's previous leading ladies.

"I was pretty convinced that I wasn't going to be able to do it, only because of the people that have played it before," she revealed to *Playbill*. "It was such a departure from anything I've ever done. I hemmed and hawed over actually accepting the role for a couple months. There was a really strong part of me that was really afraid to do it, and then I decided to do it because of how scared I was. I thought, 'Well that's reason enough to do anything.' It was definitely the biggest challenge I've ever undertaken."

The enormity of the commitment hit Sutton when she walked down 43rd Street one day, turned a corner and saw her image plastered on a huge *Anything Goes* billboard. Because the past two Broadway versions starred theater legends, the intimidated performer realized she had big shoes to fill. As a child, she owned the 1987 revival cast album and watched the musical perform on the Tony Awards.

"If I try to be Patti LuPone, I will fail miserably because there's only one," she admitted to *Broadway.com*. "But there's only one me, so I'm trying to go into it with a really open mind!"

"Reno was always a dream role," she continued. "I still can't believe it's happening. I'm going to get into rehearsals very soon. It's all going to be happening. I'm very excited."

Sutton needn't look very far for support. Kathleen Marshall, the director and choreographer behind the latest production, felt thrilled to snag the triple threat for the revival. Her leading lady could act, sing and dance.

"(Sutton is a) phenomenal dancer," she gushed to *The Washington Post*. "It was exciting to think we could have a Reno Sweeney who could be at the center of the choreography."

"Sutton has such star-quality," the director also revealed to *Playbill*. "Reno is everybody's pal in the play—she relates to everybody—and I think Sutton has that. She has that warmth and that sense of fun, and who wouldn't want to be her best friend?"

On April 7, 2011, theatergoers jammed the Stephen Sondheim Theater for *Anything Goes'* opening night performance. Sutton sat in her backstage dressing room being prepped by Julia Roberts' personal makeup artist! Typically the actress never wore makeup unless she performed. At home, she only used night cream, eye cream and sunscreen.

Upon the musical's finale, the audience offered the hard-working cast a well-deserved standing ovation. Sutton, Joel Grey, Laura Osnes, Colin Donnell and ensemble members beamed with happiness and appreciation. Long hours of demanding rehearsals had paid off nicely.

At the opening night party, guests celebrated aboard the docked USS Intrepid on the Hudson River. Notable attendees included: Jane Alexander, Charles Grodin, Zach Braff, Blair Brown, Jennifer Grey and Ron Liebman. When Sutton arrived for the festivities, partygoers burst into thunderous applause. The warm reception touched her.

"I feel stunned, amazed, thrilled, relieved, exhausted, enthusiastic," she told *Broadway.com*. "I feel everything."

Ticketholders weren't the only people buzzing about Sutton's performance. Critics gave *Anything Goes* superb reviews. They especially praised the show's unparalleled star.

"Ms. Foster has the voice of a trumpet and a big, gleaming presence that floods the house. When she leads the show-stopping "Blow, Gabriel, Blow," you figure that if no horn-tooting archangel appears, it's only because he's afraid of the competition." - *The New York Times*

"Sutton Foster doesn't just deliver those Cole Porter hits, she knocks 'em out of the park." – *Variety*

"Putting her stamp on the oh-so-juicy role of Reno, the Tony-winning Foster lets loose the brassy dame lurking behind her wholesome prettiness. While she's at it, she belts, waltzes, taps, clowns and sizzles, and makes "You're the Top" and "I Get a Kick Out of You" sound delicious." - *The New York Daily News*

"In this Roundabout production, (Sutton is) doing what she was born to do, which is headline a splashy old-fashioned musical. She can croon sweetly, belt with the best of them or sock across a comedy number. A real-deal triple threat, she can also lead the most taxing of dance routines, matching the athletic chorus kids kick for kick." – *The Hollywood Reporter*

Despite widespread acclaim for her performance, Sutton also received disappointing news during *Anything Goes'* run. Her longtime dresser Julien announced that he was moving to Massachusetts to pursue his dream of becoming an artist. Although Sutton supported her good friend, she felt devastated about losing him. The pair had chatted endlessly in dressing rooms over the years. He'd been her dresser for every major Broadway show since *Millie*. She called him a best friend and a good luck charm. Prior to every performance, she kissed his cheek before assuming her starting position.

In other news, Sutton began dating actor Bobby Cannavale. The pair met months earlier while appearing together in the off-Broadway play *Trust*. Not only did the couple enjoy one another's company, they greatly admired each other's creative talents, too. Their relationship soon became the talk of Broadway.

ANYTHING GOES
(Jennifer Tse)

One evening Patti LuPone attended an *Anything Goes* performance. The living legend then popped backstage and congratulated Broadway's latest Reno Sweeney. Sutton nearly pinched herself in disbelief while chatting with her hero. At one point she grabbed her cell phone and begged Patti to pose for a photo with her. Months later, President Bill Clinton and his daughter Chelsea caught a show, too! The former Commander-in-Chief and First Daughter praised Sutton's performance and asked to meet her.

Anything Goes also toured the talk show circuit. The cast performed numbers on *Good Morning America*, *The View*, *CBS Early Show* and *Late Night with Jimmy Fallon*. When Sutton and her co-stars gave a rousing rendition of "Blow, Gabriel, Blow" on *Late Show with David Letterman*, they left the talk show host practically speechless.

KATHLEEN MARSHALL
(Laurence Agron/PR Photos)

On the morning of the Tony nominations, Sutton mistakenly set her alarm for the wrong time. When she finally awoke, organizers had already announced the award hopefuls. The sleepy actress looked at her phone and saw a text from her brother offering his congratulations. She later read an email from her mother.

"Congratulations on your nomination," Helen wrote. "Now go find a pretty dress and get your hair cut!"

Best Actress in a Leading Role in a Musical

Sutton Foster
Anything Goes

Beth Leavel
Baby It's You!

Patina Miller
Sister Act

Donna Murphy
The People in the Picture

Anything Goes received a whopping nine nominations, including Best Revival of a Musical. Show captain Kathleen Marshall netted direction and choreography nods, while Adam Godley received Best Featured Actor in a Musical recognition. The revival also scored nominations in scenic, costume, lighting and sound categories.

The night before the 65th Tony Awards®, Sutton and her girlfriends splurged a little and rented a hotel room. They ordered in food and chatted about fun, mindless topics. The nominated actress also reflected on her charmed year. She never took her good fortune for granted and always acknowledged her blessings.

"It's been a great year," she remarked happily. "It's sort of overwhelming. Life is good."

"I'm super excited about Sunday," she added. "I have a really cool dress."

The next afternoon, Sutton perfected her makeup and hair with the help of friends. She then slipped into a Michael Kors designer dress. The elegant floor-length olive gown flattered her slim figure and magnificent skin tone.

"It's very different from anything I've ever worn," she remarked. "I like it a lot."

During the Tony Awards telecast, Joel Grey introduced the *Anything Goes* cast, and they performed the inspiring title song. Moments later, Daniel Radcliffe presented the award for Best Actress in a Musical. The winner? Sutton, of course, and she delivered a truly memorable, teary acceptance speech.

"Thank you so much. I've honestly never been happier in my life. I've never been happier in my life, and I've never been happier at a job. It doesn't even feel like a job. I love going to work every day. The most incredible company of individuals and performers... All I ever wanted to be as a little girl was to be a performer, and I get to do it every night, eight times a week, and it's unbelievable."

"I just want to thank all of my teachers: Miss Cindy and Miss Diane and Miss Juliana and Mr. Bodick. Oh gosh, and especially Larry Moss, who really helped me find this role. I want to thank Kathleen Marshall for thinking of me to play this part and for being our fearless incredible leader for the Roundabout. For Sydney and Todd for believing in me even when I didn't believe that I could play this part. I want to thank my three leading men. Joel Grey, I love you so much.

TONY AWARDS LUNCHEON
(Laurence Agron/PR Photos)

Colin Donnell and Adam Godley, it is a pleasure to fall in love with you every night."

"I have three dates this evening… My love Bobby Cannavale, who has changed my life, his incredible son Jake, who I am honored to be in his life, and my dresser Julien Havard who has been my dresser for nine years. We've done six shows together and he's leaving me next week, which is a great thing because he's pursuing his dream as an artist. He's an incredible artist. He's the word's greatest artist, and he's moving to Cape Cod, and he's going to be amazing, and I love you so much, so thank you."

When Sutton returned to *Anything Goes* the following night, she received a rapturous ovation. She loved performing every second of the show. And although she deserved enormous credit for the revival's success, she routinely deferred to her director as the production's true genius.

"I've been in shows in New York, but I've never been in one that's been so received this way — not only critically, but by the audience as well," she remarked. "We feel really lucky, and it's all Kathleen Marshall. She did everything. She created these moments, and we have to deliver them. It's so cool. We're in great hands because she did all this unbelievable work, and we're up there living in the moment. It's just amazing."

TONY WINNER
(Laurence Agron/PR Photos)

Sutton won several more awards throughout *Anything Goes'* run. She took lead actress honors from the Drama Desk, Outer Critics Circle and *Broadway.com*'s Audience Awards. In addition, Sutton and *Catch Me If You Can*'s Norbert Leo Butz were named Broadway's Best Female and Male Dancers at the 29th Annual Fred & Adele Astaire Awards.

Like her previous four shows, Sutton and coworkers spent a day working on the *Anything Goes* cast recording. The grateful star always considered it an honor to sing Cole Porter's finest songs. Despite the tight schedule, she savored the creative process.

"I'm really proud that we've been able to breathe new life and freshness into a show that's been around since 1934," she told *Playbill*. "In 2011, for it to still be relevant, to still be exciting, and for audiences to still love it... I'm excited to be a part of this version."

Sutton received a huge honor the following year when Ball State University granted her an honorary Doctor of Arts degree. The college recognized her dedication to mentoring students and many accomplishments in theater. The thrilled artist delivered an inspiring commencement speech at the university's graduation ceremony.

"You have to have the courage to go with your gut and the willingness to take the smaller job," Sutton urged, "Like life, in theater it doesn't pay to have a big ego. No job should be too small for you."

"If I didn't take the understudy position because I was too proud or felt it was beneath me, then I'm pretty sure I wouldn't be standing here in front of you today," she continued. "So say yes. Get coffee for people. Run errands. Make an impression as a hard worker. And when the opportunity arises for you to show people what you've got, show them. Who knows what can happen?"

Sutton even fulfilled a lifelong dream when she filmed a *Sesame Street* episode. In a segment on the children's show, the Broadway star demonstrated a lever to Elmo. A lifetime fan of

WITH PRESIDENT CLINTON
(Getty Images)

the educational series, she blinked in wonderment upon arriving on the set.

"It's like magic," she told *The Wall Street Journal*. "It's so pure and innocent and nostalgic. I still can count to 10 in Spanish because of *Sesame Street*."

"It's an opportunity I didn't want to miss," she continued. "It came through my agent. They called and asked about my interest and availability and I said, 'Yes, please. Done.'"

With her celebrity rising, Sutton's name even popped up on a television show. On the scripted musical drama *Smash*, a character mentioned her when listing famous theater actresses represented by a specific agent. The moment provided huge exposure on a big network.

On March 11, 2012, Sutton played her final performance as Reno Sweeney, the most demanding, fulfilling role she ever inhibited. Although Broadway's hardest working star appeared exhausted and ready to explore fresh avenues, she also felt very sad. As Sutton took her final bow, she savored the applause, basking in the moment.

"My heart feels very full," she told *Broadway.com*. "This experience has been so complete in so many ways. I have never worked with a company so wonderful, generous, hard working and joyful. I will miss everyone so much, but I am also so excited about my new adventure."

Few knew, though, that Sutton's next journey would lead her all the way across the country to a Hollywood soundstage.

"Labels of any sort are frustrating, but I want to be seen as an actress who can hopefully do many things. Musical theatre is acting with singing...but it's all acting."

BUNHEADS
Chapter Eleven

Throughout her career, people repeatedly asked Sutton if she harbored any interest in doing a television show. With her good looks, likable personality and quick humor, the popular actress seemed like a natural fit for a weekly series.

"If it was an awesome character in a show I really felt passionate about, then definitely," she told *Playbill*. "I want to do projects that I like and feel strongly about. And so far that has been stage work. But if something came along my path and it was TV or film and it excited me — then sign me up."

The right opportunity presented itself one day when *Gilmore Girls* creator Amy Sherman-Palladino contacted Sutton's agent. Having seen *Anything Goes*, the offbeat television writer felt the two-time Tony winner would make a perfect fit for her upcoming pilot. Could they meet for lunch?

Sutton adored the cult-hit *Gilmore Girls*. The dramedy featured fully fleshed characters, hilarious pop culture references and fast-tongued, screwball comedy dialogue. Yes. Yes! Yes, she would love to meet Amy.

The two women met at a New York restaurant, and Sutton kept her internal promise to behave professionally. In reality, she had a million questions for Amy but she never asked them for fear of annoying the esteemed writer. When the women parted ways, the smitten fan laughed in disbelief. Had she really just met *Gilmore Girls'* creator?

Two weeks later, Sutton's agent gave her exciting news. *ABC Family*, the network producing Amy's latest show, requested she audition for the pilot in California. The overwhelmed actress only learned details about the show after arriving in Los Angeles.

Bunheads chronicles a Las Vegas showgirl who impulsively marries a man and accompanies him to quaint Paradise, California. She finds work teaching at her mother-in-law's dance studio while adjusting to quirky small-town life.

WITH AMY SHERMAN-PALLADINO
(ABC, Inc.)

The show borrows its title from ballet's trademark upswept hairstyle.

Unlike most dance-oriented Hollywood projects, *Bunheads* didn't employ stunt doubles. Four unknown dancers depicted the young ballerinas. Meanwhile, *Gilmore Girls* alumna Kelly Bishop, Sutton's *Anything Goes* co-star, played the nemesis mother-in-law. The show's creator knew ballet intimately and always yearned to set a show in its world.

"I spent 20 years of my life with my hair in a bun," Amy remarked. "I was supposed to be a dancer. My mother was a dancer. Her greatest heartbreak was when I got on *Roseanne*. So, while writing this will never equal playing Rumpelteazer in a bus-and-truck tour of *Cats*, it does let me to tip my hat to a really special time in my life."

Sutton read for the showgirl turned ballet mentor Michelle Simms. The goofball character needed a pretty actress who could dance exceptionally well, charm the citizens of Paradise, deliver lightning-fast quips, show a dorky vulnerability and make men swoon. In other words, the part perfectly suited Broadway's favorite leading lady.

When Sutton entered the audition room, Amy, the shows' producers and network executives waited with anticipation. Ever the professional, Sutton quickly gathered her nerves and nailed the reading. Upon being offered the role, she burst into tears of joy and relief, as she had ten years earlier when she'd won the role of Millie.

Cast and crew shot *Bunheads'* pilot in November 2011. Sutton starred alongside four young ladies who delivered wisecracks as effortlessly as they performed pirouettes. Acting newcomer Julia Goldani Telles played Sasha, a gifted ballerina whose ego nearly eclipses her talent. Emma Dumont captured Melanie's cynicism, Kaitlyn Jenkins unearthed Boo's insecurity and Bailey Buntain nailed lovesick Ginnie.

Although Sutton battled nerves regarding her first major television role, she completely trusted Amy's guidance. In the meantime, she polished her classical dance skills with a private instructor, while producers installed a ballet barre in her dressing room. The determined actress found the physical demands frustrating but incredibly rewarding.

Amy's trademark fast-paced dialogue also challenged Sutton. Because of the quick exchanges, *Bunheads'* scripts were nearly double the size of a typical hour-long show. The new TV star spent hours memorizing the taxing conversation-filled scenes, often ending every day mentally and physically exhausted.

Fortunately, *ABC Family* loved *Bunheads'* charming pilot. They issued a ten-episode order, and the series' team immediately set to work. Meanwhile, the family-friendly network began creating promotional works for their latest show.

"I'm waiting for the world to see Sutton Foster," Amy proudly remarked. "I sound like a complete broken record."

"I think (Amy's) a genius," Sutton told *Playbill.* "If she would have me, I would work with her for the rest of my life."

"She's that smart and witty in real life," she continued. "She's fun, passionate and very, very hands-on, which is exciting. This is her show. She's there every single day. It's cool to be a part of something where there's such a clear voice."

AS MICHELLE IN BUNHEADS
(ABC, Inc.)

A walking pop-culture encyclopedia, Amy peppered her scripts with obscure wisecracks. Sutton admitted that the writer's references often eluded her. Sometimes during read-throughs the star asked for clarifications.

"You don't know what that means?" Amy always replied incredulously.

Sutton usually responded with exaggerated shame. After a while, though, she combed scripts for unfamiliar terms and then Googled their meanings. The dedicated star worked to keep pace with the witty writer.

The two women became fast friends off the set, too. Amy and her husband Daniel, also a writer, became Sutton's personal tour guide. The couple took their star on many sightseeing trips around Los Angeles.

"I love the vibe out here — the sunshine," Sutton told *Playbill.* "I have a backyard, and my dog Linus can play there. I love having a car and it's nice having a different lifestyle. Although I do miss New York."

Bunheads' debut date, June 11, 2012, fittingly fell on the night after the Tony Awards. Sutton felt understandably tense all afternoon. She hoped both longtime theater fans and traditional television viewers would embrace her foray into a different medium.

"In a way, I'm starting at the beginning," Sutton told *Women's Wear Daily* "I'm not known in the TV field. I hope my theater fans will find me. I'll be in their living rooms every week."

Early reviews heralded *Bunheads*. It rated as one of the best-reviewed shows of the entire season. Even the crankiest critics seemed smitten with the show's crisp dialogue, charming acting and fun characters.

"*Bunheads* is so unexpected and charming that watching the premiere feels like the first time you ever saw, say, *Six Feet Under*. It just feels like nothing else you've seen on TV." – *New York Post*

"Fanny and Michelle are wisecrackers who often speak and act before thinking, which complicates their lives and makes for delightful dialogue." - *New York Daily News*

"Sutton Foster is likable, game and just as deft with all the dialogue as Lauren Graham was (in *Gilmore Girls*)." - *Salon. com*

"Foster is delightful throughout. She adjusts wonderfully to different partners and circumstances, and is never less than real, serious or joking, drunk or sober — a perfect fit for a show that, like *Gilmore Girls*, merits a wider audience than its rough outline would suggest. It's a sweet summer treat." - *Los Angeles Times*

"*Bunheads* has that elusive momentum that most TV series so easily fumble in their first episodes. It is filled with smart, wacky writing that can pivot effortlessly into emotion when it needs to and then pirouette back to lightheartedness just as quickly." – *The Washington Post*

Regardless of how people received the show, Sutton cherished working alongside a mega-talented group. A longtime Kelly Bishop fan, she had adored the actress' turn as *Gilmore Girls'* acerbic Emily. But she also admired her Tony-winning performance as Sheila in *A Chorus Line*. As an aspiring dancer and singer, Sutton nearly wore out the acclaimed musical's original cast recording.

"We have become friends and I adore her," she gushed, "She is such an amazing partner to work with!"

Sutton also loved the four young women with whom she shared the small screen, and in turn, they idolized the Tony winner. On *Bunheads'* first day, the excited girls swapped stories of watching their co-star perform on Broadway. Meanwhile, Julia revealed that several years earlier she discovered the actress' New York home address and walked by her apartment hoping to meet the theater star.

BUNHEADS CAST
(ABC, Inc.)

"They're wonderful girls," Sutton gushed to *Broadway. com.* "We work really hard, but we have a great time."

Dancing always came naturally to the actress. Not to mention, she worked very tirelessly at the craft. However, she admitted to never studying ballet as arduously as her cast mates.

"I wasn't a serious bunhead," she confessed to *Good Morning America.* "I started dancing when I was four. I ended up doing a lot of different styles of dance, tap and jazz. I'm a jack of all trades."

More importantly, Sutton loved playing such a complex character. Michelle became the adrenalin shot Paradise so desperately needed. She portrayed a goofball amid a town of angst-ridden citizens.

"She's wreaking havoc!" Sutton told *Playbill.* "But I love her because she's flawed but trying, and it's fun to play such a messy character."

"Michelle is lost and she is desperately trying to find a place or a way that she can matter," she continued. "I think she sees herself in the girls. Her own lost youth? Her own misguided path? She'd like to impart some of her own life experience onto them — those girls could become "roots" for her."

Like *Gilmore Girls, Bunheads* created passionate fans. The show never dominated Nielsen ratings, but it cultivated a fiercely loyal following. People treasured the show's smart writing and oddball characters.

Although *Bunheads* posted modest ratings numbers, the show still exposed Sutton to far more viewers than any of her past theater projects. One day, while shopping at a grocery store, she realized several 10-year-olds were following her. They watched the actress from a distance with their mouths agape.

"You go after her," one girl urged to another.

"No, you go after her!" another whispered.

Sutton giggled quietly while pretending she couldn't hear the fans' loud chattering. Finally, a brave girl took a big breath and stepped forward.

"Are you on *Bunheads*?" she asked.

"I am," Sutton smiled.

Her friendly response diminished any fear the girls possessed. Soon they encircled her, chattering excitedly.

"Oh my gosh! I told you!" squealed one girl.

"I love that show!" shrieked another.

Sutton's fan base surprisingly ran more diverse than she ever imagined. Young girls admired her like always. However, she also received fan mail from grown men and women, who also counted themselves among her fans.

Sutton even enjoyed newfound attention from more mainstream outlets. She gave her first major talk show interview on *The Late Late Show with Craig Ferguson*. Her appearance was such a hit that the host invited her back for a second taping. The *Bunheads* star also garnered a 2012 Teen Choice Award nomination for Breakout Female Star.

Bunheads carried an intense work schedule, including many 15-hour days. However it offered Sutton many free weekends, a perk unavailable in the theater world. She utilized her free time by exploring California, including a Napa wine tasting tour and a relaxing few days in Santa Barbara.

"All I've known is eight shows a week," she explained to *The Washington Post*. "I've never known the concept of a weekend, or the concept of a hiatus."

At the start of every workday, though, she cherished arriving on the *Bunheads* set. When she wasn't creating comedy gold, she hung out in her comfy dressing room with a "Dr. Sutton Foster" sign hanging on the door. One could always find Linus chilling on the couch next to an "I Love My Dog" sign adorning a table lamp. The show's soundstage felt like a second home, and her cast members had become family.

Speaking of family, Sutton experienced a huge thrill when Hunter joined the show as - you guessed it - Michelle's brother. Her older sibling played restless Scotty Simms, who shared a strong bond with his younger sister. While he filmed his first episode, the oldest Foster child stayed at his little sister's house in Los Angeles.

"People ask me what's better, Broadway or TV? I can't pick. That's not fair," Sutton told *Broadway.com*. "*Bunheads* has been a great challenge and something I needed creatively. If Broadway will have me, I'll be back for the rest of my life."

Sutton paused for a moment. Her expressive brown eyes were temporarily lost in a memory.

"I am still the 15-year-old kid sitting at home watching the Tony Awards saying, 'I can do that.'" she insisted. "I'm still that person."

ESSENTIAL LINKS

The Official Site of Sutton Foster
www.suttonfoster.com

Sutton's Official Facebook Page
www.facebook.com/suttonlfoster

Sutton's Official Twitter Account
www.twitter.com/sfosternyc

Linus' Official Twitter Account
www.twitter.com/LalaLinus

Bunheads Blog – Musings from a Fan
www.bunheadsblog.com

Bunheads Official Website
www.twitter.com/abcfBunheads

The Tony Awards
www.tonyawards.com

Broadway.com
www.broadway.com

Hunter Foster – Official Twitter
www.twitter.com/Hunter_Foster

Playbill
www.playbill.com

Talkin' Broadway
www.talkinbroadway.com

DISCOGRAPHY

Over the Moon
The Broadway Lullaby Project

Anything Goes
Broadway Revival

An Evening With Sutton Foster
Live

The Battery's Down
Season 2

Shrek: The Musical
Broadway Cast

Wish
by Sutton Foster

Keys
The Music of Scott Alan

Young Frankenstein
Broadway Cast

The Odd Potato
The Broadway Album

The Drowsy Chaperone
Broadway Cast

Jule Styne in Hollywood
2006

The Broadway Musicals of 1926
2005

Little Women The Musical
Broadway Cast

The Maury Yeston Songbook

Thoroughly Modern Millie
Broadway Cast

The Scarlet Pimpernel
Broadway Cast

PERFORMANCES

STAGE

2011
Anything Goes
Broadway

2010
Trust
Off-Broadway

They're Playing Our Song
Actor's Fund Benefit Performance

Anyone Can Whistle
City Center Mainstage

2008
Shrek The Musical
Broadway

2007
Young Frankenstein
Broadway

2006
The Drowsy Chaperone
Broadway

2005
Little Women
Broadway

2004
Me and My Girl
Pittsburgh Civic Light Opera

Snoopy! The Musical
Benefit Show

2003
Chess
Actors' Fund Concert

2002
Funny Girl
Actors' Fund Concert

Thoroughly Modern Millie
Broadway

2001
The Three Musketeers
American Musical Theatre of San Jose

South Pacific
Pittsburgh Civic Light Opera

2000
Dorian
Goodspeed Opera House

1998
What the World Needs Now
Old Globe Theatre

Les Misérables
Broadway/ National Tour

1997
The Scarlet Pimpernel
Broadway

Annie
Broadway

1996
Grease
National Tour/Broadway

1993
The Will Rogers Follies
National Tour

1989-1993
Oklahoma!
Troy High School

Grease
Troy High School

A Chorus Line
Troy High School

Camelot
Troy High School

1987
Grease
Augusta Community Theater

1985
Annie
Augusta Community Theater

1983
A Christmas Carol
Community Theatre

PERFORMANCES

TELEVISION

2013
Home & Family

2012
Bunheads
Royal Pains
The Late Late Show
with Craig Ferguson (November)
The Late Late Show
with Craig Ferguson (August)
Late Night with Jimmy Fallon
Project Runway All Stars
The Rosie Show

2011
Sesame Street
The 65th Annual Tony Awards
The Late Show
with David Letterman

2010
Law & Order
Special Victims Unit
The Kennedy Center Honors

2009
The Battery's Down
The 63rd Annual Tony Awards
The View

2008
The Late Show
with David Letterman
Just in Case

2007
The Today Show
Flight of the Conchords
Johnny and the Sprites

2006
The 60th Annual Tony Awards

2005
The 59th Annual Tony Awards
The Early Show
The Today Show
Breakfast with the Arts

2003
A Makeover Story
The 56th Annual Tony Awards
The Today Show
The Early Show
The View
The Rosie O'Donnell Show

2002
Macy's Thanksgiving Day
Parade
The 56th Annual Tony Awards

1990
Star Search

ABC PRESS TOUR
(Andrew Evans/PR Photos)

ABOUT THE AUTHOR

Christine Dzidrums holds a bachelor's degree in Theater Arts from California State University, Fullerton. She previously wrote the biographies: *Joannie Rochette: Canadian Ice Princess, Yuna Kim: Ice Queen, Shawn Johnson: Gymnastics' Golden Girl, Nastia Liukin: Ballerina of Gymnastics, Gabby Douglas: Golden Smile, Golden Triumph* and *The Fab Five: the 2012 U.S. Women's Gymnastics Team.* Her first novel, *Cutters Don't Cry*, won a 2010 Moonbeam Children's Book Award in the Young Adult Fiction category. She also wrote the tween book, *Fair Youth,* and the beginning reader books, *Timmy and the Baseball Birthday Party* and *Timmy Adopts a Girl Dog.* Christine also authored the picture book, *Princess Dessabelle Makes a Friend.* She recently competed her second novel, *Kaylee: The 'What If?' Game* and received a second Moonbeam Children's Book Award for her biography on Miss Douglas.

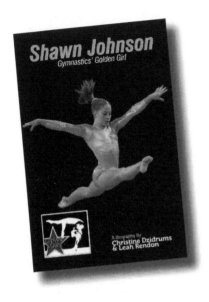

Shawn Johnson, the young woman from Des Moines, Iowa, captivated the world at the 2008 Beijing Olympics when she snagged a gold medal on the balance beam.

Shawn Johnson: Gymnastics' Golden Girl, the first volume in the **GymnStars** series, chronicles the life and career of one of sport's most beloved athletes.

Widely considered America's greatest gymnast ever, **Nastia Liukin** has inspired an entire generation with her brilliant technique, remarkable sportsmanship and unparalleled artistry.

A children's biography, *Nastia Liukin: Ballerina of Gymnastics* traces the Olympic all-around champion's ascent from gifted child prodigy to queen of her sport.

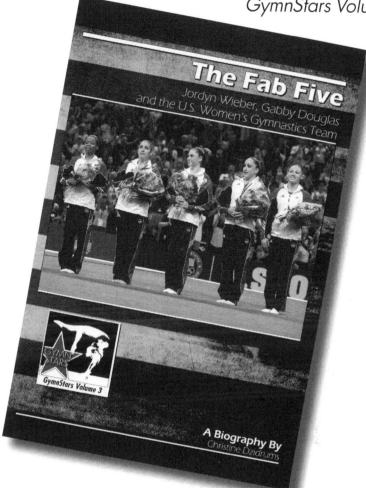

Meet the five gymnasts who will represent the United States at the 2012 London Olympics. *The Fab Five: Jordyn Wieber, Gabby Douglas and the U.S. Women's Gymnastics Team* tells each team member's life story as they rose from young gymnasts with big dreams to become international superstars of their sport. Discover the stories of **Jordyn Wieber**, **Gabby Douglas**, **McKayla Maroney**, **Aly Raisman** and **Kyla Ross** as they aim for gold in London!.

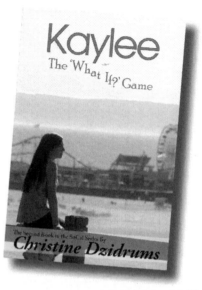

2010 Moonbeam Children's Book Award Winner! In a series of raw journal entries written to her absentee father, a teenager chronicles her penchant for self-harm, a serious struggle with depression and an inability to vocally express her feelings.

"I play the 'What If?'" game all the time. It's a cruel, wicked game."

Meet free spirit Kaylee Matthews, the most popular girl in school. But when the teenager suffers a devastating loss, her sunny personality turns dark as she struggles with debilitating panic attacks and unresolved anger. Can Kaylee repair her broken spirit, or will she forever remain a changed person?

Meet **Princess Dessabelle**, a spoiled, lonely princess with a quick temper. When she orders a kind classmate to be her friend, she learns the true meaning of friendship.

At the 2010 Vancouver Olympics, tragic circumstances thrust **Joannie Rochette** into the international spotlight when her mother died two days before the ladies short program. The world held their breath for the bereaved figure skater when she competed in her mom's memory. Joannie then captured hearts everywhere by courageously skating two moving programs to win the Olympic bronze medal. *Joannie Rochette: Canadian Ice Princess* profiles the popular figure skater's moving journey.

Meet figure skating's biggest star: **Yuna Kim**. The Korean trailblazer produced two legendary performances at the 2010 Vancouver Olympic Games to win the gold medal in convincing fashion. *Yuna Kim: Ice Queen*, the second book in the **Skate Stars** series, uncovers the compelling story of how the beloved figure skater overcame poor training conditions, various injuries and numerous other obstacles to become world and Olympic champion.

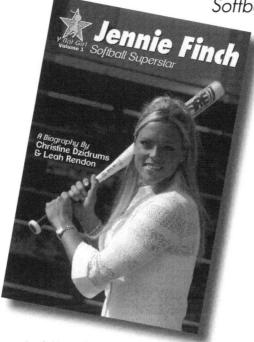

Jennie Finch fell in love with baseball as a four-year-old when her mother started taking her to Dodger games. A year later, her parents signed her up for softball lessons and the young girl was instantly smitten. As a youngster, Jennie dominated travel softball and later became a star player at La Mirada High School in Southern California. During her time at University of Arizona, she set an NCAA record with 60 consecutive wins. Blessed with remarkable pitching ability, good looks and role-model sportsmanship, Jennie became a breakout celebrity at the 2004 Athens Olympics, where she captured gold with her team. *Jennie Finch: Softball Superstar* details the California native's journey as she rose from a shy youngster playing in a t-ball league to becoming softball's most famous face, a devoted mother of two and a legend in women's sports.

BUILD YOUR TIMMY™
Collection Today!

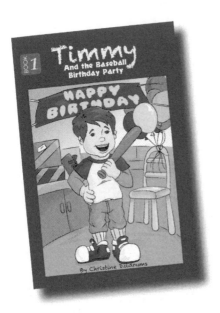

Meet 4½ year old Timmy Martin! He's the biggest baseball fan in the world.

Imagine Timmy's excitement when he gets invited to his cousin's birthday party. Only it's not just any old birthday party... It's a baseball birthday party!

Timmy and the Baseball Birthday Party is the first book in a series of stories featuring the world's most curious little boy!

Timmy Martin has always wanted a dog. Imagine his excitement when his mom and dad agree to let him adopt a pet from the animal shelter. Will Timmy find the perfect dog? And will his new pet know how to play baseball?

Timmy Adopts A Girl Dog is the second story in the series about the world's most curious 4½ year old.

Twelve-year-old Emylee Markette has felt invisible her entire life. Then one fateful afternoon, three beautiful sisters arrive in her sleepy New England town and instantly become the most popular girls at Forest Springs Middle School. To everyone's surprise, the Fay sisters befriend Emylee and welcome her into their close-knit circle. Before long, the shy loner finds herself running with the cool crowd, joining the track team and even becoming friends with her lifelong crush.

Through it all, though, Emylee's weighed down by nagging suspicions. Why were the Fay sisters so anxious to befriend her? How do they know some of her inner thoughts? What do they truly want from her?

When Emylee eventually discovers that her new friends are secretly fairies, she finds her life turned upside down yet again and must make some life-changing decisions.

Fair Youth: Emylee of Forest Springs marks the first volume in an exciting new book series.

Made in the USA
Lexington, KY
06 April 2019